The Expected Benefits of Trade Liberalization for World Income and Development

Opening the "Black Box" of Global Trade Modeling

Antoine Bouët

Food Policy Review **8**

International Food Policy Research Institute
2033 K Street, N.W.
Washington, D.C.

International Food Policy Research Institute
2033 K Street, NW
Washington, D.C. 20006-1002, U.S.A.
Telephone +1-202-862-5600
www.ifpri.org

DOI: 10.2499/0896295109FPRev8

Library of Congress Cataloging-in-Publication Data

Bouët, Antoine.
  The expected benefits of trade liberalization for world income and development : opening the "black box" of global trade modeling / Antoine Bouët.
      p.   cm. — (Food policy review ; 8)
   Includes bibliographical references.
   ISBN 978-0-89629-510-0 (alk. paper)
   1. Free trade—Developing countries—Econometric models.
2. International trade—Econometric models. 3. Poverty—Developing countries. I. Title. II. Series.
   HF2580.9.B68   2008
   339.109172′4—dc22   2008007953

Contents

Tables

Figures

Foreword

Economists often assert that trade liberalization improves welfare and alleviates poverty. By how much? That has depended on whom you ask. As shown in this study, recent estimates of the effects of trade liberalization have diverged widely. Estimates of the increase in world welfare stemming from full trade liberalization range from 0.2 percent to 3.1 percent, and estimates of the number of people who could be lifted out of poverty range from 72 million to 440 million.

This study examines how well trade modeling captures the benefits from trade liberalization. It surveys the methods used to assess the impact of trade liberalization and it considers the extent to which such assessments diverge.

Why do the modeling results differ so widely? The study attributes the differences to the fact that models use different experiments, different data, different behavioral parameters, and different theoretical features. Author Antoine Bouët examines these explanations and concludes that overall, the benefits of trade liberalization have recently been revised downward because direct trade barriers are smaller than some experts previously thought. Yet he convincingly shows that trade liberalization improves welfare and alleviates poverty, and he offers policy recommendations to help ensure that trade agreements are beneficial for developing countries' welfare and economic development. He also points to areas where further research could help clarify policy options. Of course, not all poor people gain from trade liberalization. Social policy needs to accompany trade liberalization, and more research on institutional innovation is needed for getting this done effectively.

Joachim von Braun
Director General, IFPRI

Acknowledgments

I am indebted to Hedi Bchir, Yvan Decreux, Lionel Fontagné, Jean-Louis Guérin, and Sebastien Jean, all valuable and friendly colleagues from the Centre d'Etudes Prospectives et d'Informations Internationales, Paris, who served on the "MIRAGE/MacMap" team from February 2000 to January 2005.

I am also grateful to Valdete Berisha, Caesar Cororaton, Ashok Gulati, Alex McCalla, Simon Mevel, David Orden, Alberto Valdes, participants in a seminar at the International Food Policy Research Institute on September 16, 2005, and two anonymous referees for their helpful comments and suggestions. Special thanks go to Alex McCalla for helpful and stimulating discussions. Of course all errors are mine.

Abbreviations

AGOA	African Growth Opportunity Act
CEPII	Centre d'Etudes Prospectives et d'Informations Internationales
CES	constant elasticity of substitution
CET	constant elasticity of transformation
CGE	computable general equilibrium
CGEM	computable general equilibrium model
DDA	Doha Development Agenda
EBA	Everything but Arms
EFTA	European Free Trade Area
FDI	foreign direct investment
GDP	gross domestic product
GSP	Generalized System of Preferences
GTAP	Global Trade Analysis Project
HRT	Harrison, Rutherford, and Tarr model
IMPACT	International Model for Policy Analysis of Agricultural Commodities and Trade
IQTR	inside quota tariff rate
LDC	least-developed country
LES-CES	linear expenditure system–constant elasticity of substitution
MFN	most-favored-nation
MIRAGE	modeling international relations under applied general equilibrium
NAFTA	North American Free Trade Agreement
OECD	Organisation for Economic Co-operation and Development
OQTR	outside quota tariff rate
R&D	research and development

SACU	Southern African Customs Union
SDT	special and differentiated treatment
TRQ	tariff rate quota
WTO	World Trade Organization
WYDIWYG	what you do is what you get

Introduction

Trade liberalization is expected to act positively on world economic development and poverty alleviation, both of which have become high priorities of the international community. This emphasis explains why numerous studies have focused on assessing the expected benefits of trade liberalization on development. The main empirical tools for these assessments have been the use of spatial and nonspatial partial equilibrium models, gravity equations, and single- and multi-country computable general equilibrium models (CGEMs). Multicountry CGEMs, however, have produced strikingly divergent results. As demonstrated by recent studies, the associated increase in world welfare from full trade liberalization ranges from 0.2 to 3.1 percent—results that differ by a factor of 15!

The objective of this study is to examine the efficiency of trade modeling in capturing the benefits from trade liberalization. It provides a survey of methodologies utilized to assess the impact of trade liberalization, putting an emphasis on multicountry CGEMs, and examines the extent to which such assessments diverge. The survey also demonstrates the benefits of "complementary analysis," which utilizes different methodologies to study a specific topic.

The report presents global modeling results using a general equilibrium model—the modeling international relations under applied general equilibrium (MIRAGE) model—the results of which are compared to those obtained in recent studies. Using the MIRAGE model,[1] full trade liberalization is estimated to increase world real income by US$100 billion (+0.33 percent) after 10 years of implementation. This trade reform would be development-friendly, as it entails a larger growth rate of real income for developing countries and especially for least-developed countries.

[1]The MIRAGE model was developed at the Centre d'Etudes Prospectives et d'Informations Internationales (CEPII), Paris. A full description of the model is available at the CEPII website (www.cepii.fr).

The report offers four explanations on the divergent results of multicountry general equilibrium models, including the MIRAGE study undertaken here:

1. experiments are not the same;
2. data are not the same;
3. behavioral parameters are not the same; and
4. theoretical features are not the same.

Each explanation is examined in detail. The simulation in this report is also utilized to check explanations of divergent results in the literature. To quantify the importance of the four factors, a sensitivity analysis is carried out. This method provides a quantitative assessment of expected benefits from liberalization when one hypothesis is modified, and it confirms that:

*   Direct trade barriers, such as tariffs, tariff quotas, and antidumping duties, are smaller than previously expected. Consequently, the expected benefits from full trade liberalization are not as large as assessed in recent literature.
*   In multicountry trade models, the size of the expected benefits depends crucially on the value of Armington trade elasticities. The simulation that has been carried out in this study is founded on the Global Trade Analysis Project elasticities, which are small compared to others used in the literature.
*   The size of expected benefits from trade liberalization also depends crucially on the potential positive impact of trade openness on factor productivity. Several multicountry trade models utilize ad hoc methodologies to capture this element, such as a relation that automatically amplifies expected benefits, but these methodologies do not explain how trade integration raises factor productivity.

Benefits from eliminating tariff barriers, domestic support, and export subsidies have been recently revised downward; nevertheless, trade liberalization is beneficial and could contribute to poverty alleviation.

Chapter 1

Background

Development and poverty alleviation have become high priorities of the international community. One of the key objectives of the Millennium Development Goals, set forth by the United Nations for 2015, is a reduction by half of the number of people living on less US$1.00 per day. But the world poverty headcount was stagnant in absolute terms during the 1990s. In 2003, nearly one-quarter of the world population was living on less than US$1.00 per day, and one-half on less than US$2.00 per day. To emphasize the need to combat these high poverty levels, the current global trade negotiations conducted by the World Trade Organization (WTO) are referred to as the Doha Development Agenda (DDA).

Although recent literature confirms the positive relationship between liberalization and poverty alleviation, it also emphasizes that the relationship is complex. Winters, McCulloch, and McKay (2004) and Reimer (2002) identify several key linkages between liberalization and poverty alleviation, such as the price and availability of goods, factor prices, government transfers, incentives for investment and innovation, evolution of terms of trade, and short-term risk.

The traditional argument in favor of a positive relationship between trade liberalization and poverty focuses on the first two linkages. Many poor people are working in the agricultural sector, where trade distortions are particularly high. Liberalization could imply higher world agricultural prices and could raise activity and remunerations in this sector in the Third World. The same beneficial outcome could also occur in the textiles and wearing apparel sectors, where protection remains high and developing countries have a comparative advantage.

Nevertheless, openness might lead to negative outcomes. First, the decrease in import duties might reduce custom revenues so that the government's public receipts may be cut and government transfers can shrink. Second, terms of trade can be negatively affected, either because import prices increase or export prices decrease from more severe competition in export markets. Third, cutting trade barriers in a country increases import competition, which implies reallocation of productive factors and entails adjustment costs and short-term risk.

Furthermore, this positive relationship between trade liberalization and poverty is based on the predominance of agricultural activities in developing countries. But not all developing countries have a comparative advantage in agriculture, and not all poor people are engaged in agricultural activities. In fact, benefits for the poor are expected from trade liberalization, but adverse effects can also occur in the short and the long run, which explains why numerous studies have focused on whether gains outweigh losses. Some of the analytical instruments used here are

- spatial and nonspatial partial equilibrium trade models, which study in detail equilibrium in some markets without consideration of what happens elsewhere, by assuming that a shock in the markets under study does not significantly affect the rest of the economy;
- gravity models, which seek to explain bilateral trade flows by using the economic size of the two trading partners and the geographic distance between them; and
- single- and multicountry computable general equilibrium models (CGEMs), which consider the formation of equilibrium on all markets, supposing that a shock on a specific market may have a significant impact on all markets.

The objective of this study is to provide a survey of methodologies utilized to assess the impact of trade liberalization on developing countries and world income, with specific focus on multicountry CGEMs, and to examine the diverging results of such assessments. It is divided into five chapters. Chapter 1 consists of this overview. Chapter 2 looks at the advantages and drawbacks of each model, with a particular focus on partial and general equilibrium models. Chapter 3 undertakes global trade modeling under general equilibrium—the modeling international relations under applied general equilibrium (MIRAGE) model. Chapter 4 compares MIRAGE to other CGEMs; it is followed by a conclusion (Chapter 5).

Chapter 2 suggests that although no single method is better than others from a methodological point of view, the multicountry CGEMs are attractive analytical instruments if the objective is to analyze the global effects of multilateral trade reform. Today, this analysis can be done more easily, thanks to the availability of a complete database (the Global Trade Analysis Project [GTAP]) and the increased capabilities of computers. Although offering a consistent picture of the world economy, this analytical instrument can be utilized to evaluate the impact of trade reform on a large number of productive sectors, trading zones, and productive factors. Nevertheless, multicountry CGEMs are complex analytical instruments that necessitate highly simplified (and sometimes unrealistic) assumptions and modeling choices.

Chapter 3 undertakes global trade modeling to assess the impact of liberalization on poverty. Using the MIRAGE model full trade liberalization is expected to increase world real income by US$100 billion (+0.33 percent) after 10 years of implementation. This trade reform would be development-friendly, as it would entail a larger growth rate for developing countries, especially least-developed countries (LDCs). It could also contribute to poverty alleviation and reduce world income inequality. Nevertheless, certain developing countries might lose from this world reform because of adverse evolution of their terms of trade. Finally, this assessment highlights the major role played by agriculture and tariffs in expected benefits from liberalization.

Is the MIRAGE assessment comparable to conclusions of recent studies on the same topic? To answer this question, Chapter 4 provides a literature review of recent CGEMs. Recent assessments using CGEMs clearly highlight major divergences. From full trade liberalization, the associated increase in world welfare ranges from 0.2 to 3.1 percent (Dessus, Fukasaku, and Safadi 1999), results that differ by a factor of more than 15![1] The impact on the poverty headcount is also divergent, as the estimated number of people lifted from poverty ranges from 72 million (Anderson, Martin, and Van der Mensbrugghe 2005c) to 440 million (Cline 2004), a ratio of 6.[2] This picture is a rather diverse one of the effects of trade liberalization on poverty. Moreover, as a sophisticated and complex tool of analysis, CGEMs are often treated as "black boxes," results of which are difficult to understand.

Chapter 4 provides four different explanations for the divergent results of trade modeling:

1. Experiments are not the same. Assessing the impact of the DDA is a difficult task because of insufficient information on the contents of the final agreement and on the way countries will implement it. Even if the experiment is based on full trade liberalization, divergences could arise: does the experiment concern all distortions or only border measures? Has a pre-experiment been conducted to account for the trade shocks that occur between the database period and the

---

[1] Comparisons must be done in terms of percentages, as welfare might be defined in either 1997 or 2001 dollars.

[2] In 2003, the number of people in poverty (using the definition of less than US$2.00 per day) was estimated at 2.8 billion (World Bank 2004b). Full trade liberalization is estimated to decrease world poverty by an amount ranging from 2.5 to 15.1 percent.

implementation date of the liberalization?[3] Finally, some modeling analyses envisage fiscal policy implemented simultaneously to offset the loss of tariff receipts, whereas others do not.

2. Data are not the same. At this level, potential sources of divergent assessments are manifold: for instance, the social accounting matrix and data on economic policies. Among different assessments, the main source of divergence comes from data on market access. The data may or may not take into account all regional agreements and all preferential schemes. Tariff reduction may be imposed on bound or applied duties. Furthermore, data on the bound level of domestic support may or may not be included. Finally, sector and product decomposition can differ.

3. Behavioral parameters are not the same. A CGEM needs an estimation of several parameters. A key parameter of this modeling exercise is the trade elasticity: it measures the degree to which a change in relative prices leads to substitution of imported products for domestic products. There is a disagreement in the scientific community on the values of these parameters. The impact of liberalization on trade flows, and thus on activity, is highly sensitive to these parameters.

4. Theoretical assumptions are not the same. Models can differ in their theoretical assumptions. Labor and capital may be sector-specific or they can be reallocated to other sectors. Land supply may be fixed or may be positively related to real remuneration. Competition may be perfect or imperfect. Openness may or may not have a positive effect on factor productivity. Divergence may also concern functional forms such as utility function, and complementarity versus substitutability of productive factors and intermediate inputs or among intermediate goods.

Each explanation is examined in detail. To quantify the importance of these factors, a sensitivity analysis is carried out, which includes several specifications of the MIRAGE CGEM. This method quantifies the impact of different assumptions on results and confirms that:

• Direct trade barriers, such as tariffs, tariff quotas, and antidumping duties, are smaller than previously expected.

---

[3]For example, recent assessments study the effects of implementing liberalization in 2005, while the most recent database available is for 2001. A pre-experiment can be realized to account for different trade agreements that took place between 2001 and 2005, such as the end of the Uruguay Round, Everything but Arms, African Growth Opportunity Act, and the accession of China to the WTO. If these agreements are not accounted for, the effects of trade liberalization would be overstated.

- In multicountry trade models, the size of the expected benefits depends crucially on the value of Armington trade elasticities.[4]
- The size of expected benefits from trade liberalization also depends on the potential positive impact of trade openness on factor productivity or capital accumulation.

In addition to providing explanations of divergent results of trade modeling, this report also sums up convergent conclusions of other studies on trade liberalization and world income, which affirm that:

1. Liberalizing agriculture is the main source of expected gains, accounting for about two-thirds of global gains.
2. Tariffs are by far the main source of distortions.
3. Developing countries could greatly benefit from these reforms.
4. Liberalizing trade policies of developing countries could contribute to about half of the expected benefits.
5. Full trade liberalization could be beneficial for nearly all countries throughout the world, whereas it is quite plausible that the incomplete liberalization envisaged by the DDA could be negative for numerous developing countries, especially if it leads to special and differentiated treatment (SDT): under this WTO exception regime, developing countries are authorized not to liberalize their economy, or to do so to a lesser extent. This policy option could mean less liberalization for middle-income countries and no liberalization for LDCs.

This study does not provide any estimation of how full trade liberalization could alleviate poverty. Such an assessment would require the utilization of numerous household surveys in developing countries, which goes beyond the technical feasibilities of this survey. But another method would be feasible: using poverty elasticities, as in World Bank (2002, 2004a) or in Cline (2004). An examination of this method, however, reveals that it is founded on assumptions that are too strong: normal or lognormal internal distribution of income and constant dispersion of this distribution after the trade reform.

Furthermore, this method describes the relation between trade liberalization and poverty alleviation as a simplistic one: liberalizing trade would suffice to increase unskilled labor's remuneration in developing countries, which would automatically (and proportionally) reduce the stock of poor people in the world. This description is not realistic. Trade liberalization frequently has contrasting effects on poverty

---

[4]In trade models, Armington elasticities measure the substitutability between domestic and imported products.

(for example, differential effects on agricultural activities versus industry or services, urban versus rural, and on different levels of education). Studies on poverty alleviation have to focus on these contrasting effects and on policies—international and domestic—that must be implemented simultaneously to accompany liberalization. Finally, poverty alleviation is a highly qualitative concept, an aspect that is not accounted for in these studies.

The objective of this study is to examine the efficiency of trade modeling in capturing the benefits from trade liberalization. It is aimed at evaluating the advantages and drawbacks of different methodologies, but it is focused on multicountry CGEMs, which have received great attention in recent years from academics, development institutions, and the public in general. This methodological evaluation is founded on a new model of expected benefits from full trade liberalization, the results of which are carefully compared to those obtained in recent studies. The ultimate aim of this work is threefold:

1. to assess realistically the consequences of trade liberalization on development;
2. to understand the divergent results of recent studies; and
3. to define the role that can be played by the International Food Policy Research Institute (IFPRI) in this area.

In conclusion, Chapter 5 responds to these three issues.

Chapter 2

Methodologies for Assessing the Impact of Trade Liberalization

Several methodologies are available for evaluating the economic consequences of trade liberalization: spatial and nonspatial partial equilibrium trade analysis; two-country and multicountry general equilibrium models; and gravity models. This chapter provides an overview of these methodologies and identifies their main advantages and drawbacks. These different methodologies are presented in light of the traditional distinction made between partial and general equilibrium models.

There is no absolutely superior methodology for analyzing international trade. To understand why, keep in mind that the world of international trade is infinitely complex, involving hundreds of countries with different endowments and consumer preferences, thousands of products and their derivatives (which are either substitutable or complementary in final or intermediate inputs), and a great variety of national policy instruments. Furthermore, this world is dynamic in time.

But economists try to develop models to understand reality. Abstraction of critical elements is necessary, and models are by definition simplifications of the real world. These simplifications are made by the modeler, whose concern is to answer specific questions of particular interest.

Depending on the objective of the research, the choice of modeling type is fairly obvious. If the researcher wants to evaluate the consequences of a multilateral trade agreement on national incomes, trade, and production, a multicountry multisector general equilibrium model is appropriate. If the objective is the impact of trade liberalization on income distribution and poverty, accounting for the diversity of households' income sources and consumption structures is the key concern, and including heterogeneous households can be done in both a single- and a multi-country general equilibrium model. If the objective is to analyze the level of distortion and the consequences on trade flows in the world market of a specific commodity that is characterized by a great diversity of production systems (such as sugar or rice), a partial equilibrium model or a gravity model is needed, and so forth. Each method has both advantages and drawbacks, and the modeler has to keep in mind these specificities. Presenting these advantages and drawbacks is the objective of this chapter.

Partial Equilibrium Modeling

The main feature of a partial equilibrium model is that it does not have to consider equilibrium on all markets in order to focus on one or several markets or sectors. This approach leads to increased tractability and/or allows for more analytical detail in modeling complex policy instruments or spatially different production systems. Here I develop a very simple partial equilibrium model to explain its main features.

Consider n countries, with 1 being the domestic country and $j = 2, \ldots, n$ being the index for foreign countries. In the sector studied, imports and domestic goods are imperfect substitutes: the Armington[1] hypothesis means that products are differentiated by their country of origin. Let Q_i^D be the demanded quantity of the good studied in country i, Q_i^S the supplied quantity in country i, P_1 the domestic price of the good studied, P_j^* its foreign price in country j, t_j is the tariff applied domestically on imports of this good when it comes from country j.

Equation (1) is the demand function for domestically produced goods, and equation (2) is the demand function for imports from country j. Substitutability between products implies that demand for one product depends on all prices:

$$Q_1^D = Q_1^D(P_1; P_2; \ldots; P_n),\tag{1}$$

$$Q_j^D = Q_j^D(P_1; P_2; \ldots; P_n).\tag{2}$$

The supply of domestic good is:

$$Q_1^S = Q_1^S(P_1).\tag{3}$$

The supply of foreign goods depends on foreign prices:

$$Q_j^S = Q_j^S(P_j^*).\tag{4}$$

---

[1]See Armington (1969). This hypothesis is not a necessary one in partial equilibrium models.

The partial equilibrium model allows for supposing that the consumers' incomes and the cost of productive factors are constant.

Finally, the gap between domestic and foreign prices reflects the domestic tariff (t_j) and the cost of transportation from country j to country 1 (τ_j). The domestic tariff is indexed by j (the exporting country), as preferential schemes, regional agreements, or certain features of the protective instrument[2] can result in trade discrimination:

$$P_j = P_j^*(1 + t_j + \tau_j). \qquad (5)$$

This model is easily tractable (see the COMPAS model—Francois and Hall 1993—for a log-linear version or Francois and Hall 1997 for a constant elasticity of substitution [CES] version). This very simple model can be enriched in several directions: other goods, complementary or substitutes; intermediate goods; more complex policy instruments; strategic interactions; or asymmetric information. The specificity of this model is that it supposes that other markets are in equilibrium and that shocking this market does not affect the equilibrium on other markets (that could then affect equilibrium on this market).

The specific advantages of this type of model are its simplicity and tractability. As illustrated in the three following sections, tractability permits easy replication of calculations, while theoretical simplicity allows one to analyze specific issues more deeply, such as a complex policy instrument or production system. Nevertheless from a theoretical point of view, this model can be greatly enriched by complementarities or substitutability, intermediate goods, strategic interaction, or asymmetric information. The first advantage of partial equilibrium analysis is that it gives the researcher flexibility.

Estimating the Costs of Protection
This section illustrates the tractability of a simple partial equilibrium model. Suppose that the objective of the research is an evaluation of the costs of protection in several sectors or several economies.

Here I adopt the previous theoretical framework and add supplementary simplifications: domestic and foreign goods are perfect substitutes; there are no transportation costs, and the economy being studied is small, in the sense that any trade reform it implements has no impact on world prices. Finally, the tariff imposed is nondiscriminatory.

The welfare cost CP of a tariff t in sector i can be directly expressed from this very simple framework:

---

[2]The tariff may be specific and not ad valorem, or it can be an antidumping duty.

$$CP = (\varepsilon_S Q^S + \varepsilon_D Q^D)(t^2/2),\qquad(6)$$

where ε_S is the price elasticity of domestic production and ε_D that of domestic consumption. Equation (6) means that the cost of protection increases with the quantities demanded and supplied, the level of price elasticities, and the square of the tariff (higher tariffs are proportionally more distorting).

The quantity of this good can be normalized so that the world price is equal to 1. If the importing country is small, the economic consequences of a tariff can be derived immediately from this equation; calculating the distortion resulting from protection (variation in consumer surplus, producer surplus, and public receipt) only requires information on the level of the tariff, the levels of domestic consumption and production, and the price elasticity of demand and supply.

The Institute for International Economics has thus conducted several studies on the costs of protection with the help of this methodology (see Hufbauer and Elliott 1994 for the United States and Messerlin 2001 for the EU). It is of course a very simple theoretical framework, but it is transparent, permits decomposition into consumers/producers/fiscal gains and losses, and can be easily replicated allowing for direct international and/or intersector comparisons.

Estimating the Impact of Complex Instruments

National governments are adopting numerous and diverse policy instruments to restrict international trade, to control or modify the quality of imported products, or to guarantee domestic objectives (such as specific price levels for either consumers or producers). Partial equilibrium models are highly appropriate for analyzing these instruments.

The reference framework of partial equilibrium analysis is retained. Once again it is assumed that domestic and foreign goods are perfect substitutes, there are no transportation costs, and the economy is small. Instead of a tariff, the domestic government imposes a minimum producer price P_M. The domestic supply is now:

$$\begin{aligned} Q_1^S = \; & Q_1^S(P_M) = Q_M & \text{if} \quad P_1 \le P_M, & \qquad(7)\\ & Q_1^S(P_1) & \text{if} \quad P_1 > P_M. \end{aligned}$$

This description entails a kink in the domestic supply function, which means that there are two regimes of production. It has important consequences on the way prices and quantities adjust to an external shock, as it increases inelasticity of excess supply and/or demand on international markets (see McCalla and Josling 1985). This production function can be easily analyzed in a partial equilibrium model.

Complex policy instruments are numerous in international trade: variable import levies, quotas, minimum prices, voluntary export restraints, tariff rate quotas, sanitary and phytosanitary norms, and the like. Partial equilibrium models are extremely useful to evaluate their impacts.

Accounting for Spatially Diverse Production Systems

Spatial price equilibrium models are one of the most commonly utilized classes of agricultural models. This kind of model is designed to endogenize trade flows in a consistent way with spatial analysis. Prices in two markets are linked only if trade occurs between these two places. More precisely, according to the logic of Enke-Samuelson-Takayama-Judge model, if P_{it} is the price in place i at time t, τ_{jit} the transaction costs of spatial arbitrage from location j to location i at time t, and x_{ijt} is exported quantity from i to j. The transaction cost may be defined as a function of the prices in the two places and of transportation costs.

The rent R_{jit} of spatial arbitrage between places i and j can be defined as the benefit of exporting from j to i, that is, of buying in j, transporting the commodity from j to i, and selling in i:

$$R_{jit} = P_{it} - P_{jt} - \tau_{jit}. \tag{8}$$

Rents of spatial arbitrage are exhausted when trade occurs (trade implies that the difference in prices is equal to transportation costs); when no trade takes place, rents are negative or null (under no trade, prices are disconnected, so that exportation is not beneficial):

$$x_{jit} > 0 \quad \Rightarrow \quad R_{jit} = 0, \tag{9}$$

$$x_{jit} = 0 \quad \Rightarrow \quad R_{jit} \leq 0.$$

Putting it differently: $R_{jit} x_{jit} = 0$.

Takayama and Judge (1964) showed that this problem can be represented by the maximization of a quadratic objective function subject to a set of linear constraints (a quadratic program). Bawden (1966) and Takayama (1967) introduced trade policies into the model.

As an example of the use of this model, Devadoss et al. (2005) examine the effects of the U.S.–Canadian softwood lumber disputes on all national markets (including the United States and Canada). The model is solved under several constraints: total shipments from i to all j are not greater than quantity supplied in i; total shipments from all i to j are not smaller than quantity demanded in j; the difference in market demand price in i and market supply price in i covers transportation costs and tariffs; and demand, supply, and shipments are positive or null. This model allowed for a precise assessment of the impact of the U.S. imposition of a 27.2 percent tariff on Canadian softwood lumber on U.S., Canadian, and other markets.

A great advantage of this analytical instrument is the facility with which different policies can be introduced. A tariff is as easily implemented as in a nonspatial equilibrium model. A quantitative restriction can be introduced in a direct manner, just as for a linear inequality constraint.

I now turn to general equilibrium models.

General Equilibrium Models

The first objective of general equilibrium is to analyze how equilibrium is simultaneously determined in every market. The expansion of activity in a sector may have economy-wide effects, which can be captured by this framework but which are not systematically accounted for by partial equilibrium models. This expansion increases demand for primary factors and their remuneration; it therefore raises the cost of production for other sectors and the demand of intermediate goods addressed to other sectors. Further, it affects the level of net public receipts and/ or expenses if the production or the utilization of some factors is either taxed or subsidized; the variation of remuneration modifies the income level of households, which in turn change their levels of consumption, and so forth.

As a result of this full integration of income and interdependence effects, general equilibrium accounts for the complete budget closure of a model. If the behavior of n agents is modeled and $(n-1)$ agents are globally in budget deficit (they consume more than they produce), it ensures that the nth agent is in surplus: she or he produces more than she or he consumes; and this surplus exactly matches the global deficit of the other $(n-1)$ agents. In making this assumption, a general equilibrium model is fully consistent, but simultaneously a general equilibrium model needs simplifying assumptions about specific elements, such as policy instruments, household or government behavior, and complementarity/substitutability among productive factors. Here I present three possible applications of general equilibrium models in international trade.

Single-Country CGEM and Trade Agreements

The most direct way to account for general equilibrium effects is to construct a single-country trade model. Of course, this kind of model cannot measure bilateral trade flows, but it takes into consideration general equilibrium effects. To illustrate this method, consider one country and N sectors ($k = 1, 2, \ldots, N$). In the following simplistic structure, imported and domestic goods are perfect substitutes; there is no intermediate input in production, no government, and labor is the sole productive factor (its remuneration is w). These are uncommon features of single-country trade models used in the literature, but they allow for a concise presentation of the model in only eight equations—equations (10) through (17). Furthermore, there is perfect competition in all markets and perfect mobility of labor across sectors. The demand function of good k depends on all prices (allowing for substitutability or complementarities among goods) and national income Y, supposedly distributed to a single household whose demand is representative:

$$Q_k^D = Q_k^D(P_1; P_2 \ldots P_N; Y) = Q_k^D(P; Y). \tag{10}$$

P is a vector of N prices. The country's supply of good k is a function of the domestic price of good k and the remuneration of labor w:

$$Q_k^S = Q_k^S(P_k; w). \tag{11}$$

Let ED_k be the domestic excess demand for good k. If it is positive (negative), it represents imports (exports):

$$ED_k = Q_k^D(P; Y) - Q_k^S(P_k; w). \tag{12}$$

Let ES_k^* be the rest of the world's excess supply of good k. If it is positive (negative), it represents the exports (imports) of the rest of the world.

$$ES_k^* = ES_k^*(P_k^*). \tag{13}$$

The government applies import duties t_k on good k:

$$P_k = P_k^*(1 + t_k). \tag{14}$$

P_k might be sufficiently low for ED_k to be positive: the country imports good k, which is in excess supply in the rest of the world ($ES_k^* > 0$). Exports occur in the case of high values of P_k (the case of positive exports and positive t_k is possible; then t_k represents an export subsidy). Then ED_k and ES_k^* are negative.

Let L_k^D be the demand of labor by sector k and $\bar{L}$ the total endowment of labor. The labor market equilibrium requires:

$$\sum_{k=1}^{N} L_k^D(w; P_k) = \bar{L}. \tag{15}$$

National income comes from labor and import taxes:

$$Y = w\bar{L} + \sum_k t_k P_k^* ED_k. \tag{16}$$

It is important to note that in the case of exports, either t_k is zero or exports are subsidized (t_k is positive and ED_k is negative).

There are several ways to bring about closure of this model. One is to consider that the current account is constant; in other words, the country is unable to borrow from, or to lend to, the rest of the world:

$$-\sum_k P_k^* ED_k = \bar{CA}. \tag{17}$$

I show the advantages and drawbacks of this kind of model after having presented the multicountry general equilibrium model.

Multicountry CGEM and Trade Agreements

The previous framework is now extended to n countries ($i = 1, 2, \ldots, n$); there are still N sectors ($k = 1, 2, \ldots, N$). Products are differentiated by their country of origin (Armington 1969).

Let $CP_{k,i,j}$ be the price paid by country j's consumers when they buy good k produced in i (consumer price).[3] The demand in country j for good k produced in country i $Q^D_{k,i,j}$ depends on all consumer prices and on country j's income:

$$Q^D_{k,i,j} = (\mathbf{CP}; Y_j), \tag{18}$$

where $\mathbf{CP}$ is the vector of all consumer prices. If i is different from j, $Q^D_{k,i,j}$ represents trade flows of good k from i to j.

Let $PP_{k,i,j}$ be the price received by country i's producers when they sell good k in country j (producer price). The supply of good k produced in i to country j ($Q^S_{k,i,j}$) depends on $PP_{k,i,j}$ and the cost of labor in i:

$$Q^S_{k,i,j} = Q^S_{k,i,j}(PP_{k,i,j}; w_i). \tag{19}$$

Let $t_{k,i,j}$ be the tariff imposed by country j on good k coming from country i. The gap between producer price and consumer price is defined by:[4]

---

[3] In the case of the double country index (i, j), the first index i refers to supply; the second one j refers to demand.

[4] We could also add a transportation cost $\tau_{k,i,j}$ of good k from i to j, but it would require the modeling of a transportation sector.

$$CP_{k,i,j} = PP_{k,i,j}(1 + t_{k,i,j}).$$ (20)

If $L_{k,i}$ is the demand of labor in sector k in country i and $\bar{L}_i$ is the total supply of labor in country i, factor market equilibrium requires:

$$\sum_k L_{k,i}(w_i; PP_{k,i}) = \bar{L}_i,$$ (21)

where $PP_{k,i}$ is a component of a vector of production prices of good k in country i. Country j's national income is defined by:

$$Y_j = w_j \bar{L}_j + \sum_k \sum_{i \neq j} t_{k,i,j} PP_{k,i,j} Q^D_{k,i,j}.$$ (22)

Finally, all countries' current accounts CA are constant:

$$\sum_k \sum_{j \neq i} PP_{k,i,j} Q^S_{k,i,j} - \sum_k \sum_{j \neq i} PP_{k,j,i} Q^D_{k,j,i} = \overline{CA}_i.$$ (23)

Compared to a single-country model, the immediate advantage of a multi-country trade model is its ability to calculate bilateral trade flows. It is all the more important in a world where trade discrimination is extensive. Single-country trade models cannot really capture discriminatory effects of trade, such as regional agreements or preferential schemes.

Nonetheless, the complexity is significantly increased in multicountry models, as they add a new dimension to trade. Equations can now be four-dimensional (intermediate inputs: two sectors; two countries), and their number increases exponentially with the number of geographic zones and sectors.[5] All theoretical assumptions (households' disaggregations, imperfect competition, imperfect mobility of productive factors, unemployment, and the like) that can be applied in a single-country trade model can also be adopted in a multicountry trade model, but these extensions are constrained by computational capacity. Thus these models are complementary analytical instruments of trade liberalization: for example, multicountry trade models can evaluate the impact of regional agreements at a macroeconomic level, whereas a single-country trade model with extended disaggregation of households can use this macroeconomic shock (variation in world prices) to evaluate its distributional impact.

---

[5]That is, intermediate inputs of good k originated in country i by sector l in country j. Thus decomposing in 10 sectors and 10 geographic zones leads to $10 \times 10 \times 10 \times 10 = 10,000$ equations for intermediate inputs. But in a majority of CGE applications, the trade flows are three dimensional, because trade data in the GTAP database are in three dimensions.

For assessing the impact of trade reform, two-country or multicountry trade models need data on household consumption; sector production; value-added, intermediate inputs, exports, and imports; and data on economic policies to represent the world economy. The model is calibrated so that it represents the world economy at the initial period of time, and the trade reform is then applied.

CGEMs are thus consistent representations of the world economy, but adopting this theoretical framework is costly in terms of economic data, information on behavioral parameters, and computational time. The modeler is therefore committed to simplifying assumptions.

Gravity Models

The gravity equation has been an attractive analytical tool for researchers in the international trade area, as its utilization has been manifold. Gravity equations can be utilized to evaluate market access, border effects, trading potentials, the impact of regional agreements, and so forth.

Yet the first generation of gravity equations had no solid theoretical foundation; they were intuitively appealing for explaining international trade through attractive forces (activity in the exporting zone, demand in the importing one) and resistive forces (transportation costs, trade barriers, and the like). Fortunately, the gravity equation has received specific theoretical attention in the works of Anderson (1979), Bergstrand (1989, 1990), Deardorff (1998), Anderson and van Wincoop (2003) and is now well founded.

Consider a gravity equation following the theoretical model of Fontagné, Pajot, and Pasteels (2001): in a general equilibrium model, all goods are differentiated by place of origin and each region is producing only one good. The supply of each good is fixed. Consumers have identical and homothetic preferences represented by a CES utility function.

I adopt the following notations. The value of exports from i to j is x_{ij}, y_i is country i's total income and y^W is the world income, α_i are weights, s_k is the share of country k in world income, and $(\tau_{ij} - 1)$ measures trade costs. Trade costs might be seen only as direct costs resulting from transportation and taxation at the border. They might also include information costs on quality, technical features, and availability of the product. Finally, σ is the elasticity of substitution between all goods.

The following expression can be drawn from this model:

$$x_{ij} = \frac{1}{\tau_{ij}} \frac{y_i y_j}{y^W} \frac{\left(\dfrac{\tau_{ij}}{\widetilde{\Pi}_j} \right)^{1-\sigma}}{\sum_k s_k \left(\dfrac{\tau_{ik}}{\widetilde{\Pi}_k} \right)^{1-\sigma}}, \qquad (24)$$

where

$$\tilde{\Pi}_j = \left[\sum_i \alpha_i \tau_{ij}^{\,1-\sigma} \right]^{\frac{1}{1-\sigma}} \qquad (25)$$

is a CES index of the rate of trade costs when acceding to country j. The meaning of the gravity equation (24) is intuitive and straightforward. Exports from i to j are positively related to the supply capacity of i (i's income), the demand capacity of j (j's income)—these are the attractive forces—and negatively related to trade costs.

Compared to the gravity equation expressed in McCallum (1995) and Wall (1999), a new insight is the inclusion of not only absolute trade costs (τ_{ij}) but also of relative trade costs—see the numerator of the third fraction in equation (24). Consider the case of trade flows from New Zealand to Australia: they are larger because the absolute geographic distance between the two countries is smaller, but also because the importing country is remote from all other countries in the world. Considering that the level of bilateral protection is fixed, increased protection of Australia on products coming from the rest of the world strengthens trade flows from New Zealand.

The advantage of the gravity equation is its extreme tractability. Furthermore, it gives very positive econometric results. Nevertheless, it explains only exports, even though in a tentative (but not convincing) effort, Wall (1999) tries to draw welfare costs associated with protection from a gravity equation; he tests econometrically a nonmicroeconomically founded equation, utilizes a weakly founded index of trade policy, and derives welfare effects by applying a proportion rule to the trade effect.

In concluding this methodological review, it is important to note that these analytical instruments are complementary, not global substitutes. Multicountry general equilibrium models are comprehensive and consistent analytical tools for evaluating the consequences of trade liberalization: they account for income effects, interdependence among factor and product markets, discriminatory aspects of international trade, and so forth. Nevertheless, they are complex and demanding in terms of statistical information. Furthermore, they cannot fully reflect the complexity of national economies, because the modeler is bound to simplify theoretical representation to simultaneously account for international trade relations with other geographic zones. On the other hand, partial equilibrium models offer less consistency and are less extensive, but they give the modeler more freedom to study a specific aspect of trade liberalization. They are an excellent instrument to analyze complex behavior (such as strategic interaction or asymmetric information), complicated production systems, or intricate policy instruments. For example, IFPRI's International Model for Policy Analysis of Agricultural Commodities and Trade (IMPACT) is an international partial equilibrium analysis that can assess the effects of population, investment and trade scenarios, and more recently of long-term change in water demand

Table 2.1   Comparisons of types of models

Characteristic	Nonspatial partial equilibrium	Spatial partial equilibrium	Single-country CGE	Multicountry CGE	Gravity equation
Flexibility and/or tractability	***	**	**	*	**
Degree of realism	**/***	**/***	**	*	**
Accounting for interdependence and real income effects	*	*	**	***	**
Complex policy instruments	***	**	**	*	**
Concern with overall impact of global changes in levels of protection	*	*	*	***	*
Concern with implications of policy or shipping rate changes across many commodities	***	***	*	*	***
Concern with impact on income distribution	*	*	**	**	—

Notes: Models are ranked from * (least applicable) to *** (most applicable) in terms of their applicability to each characteristic listed. CGE, computed general equilibrium; — indicates not applicable.

and availability on food security and nutrition status. This model can clearly cover a large scope of research issues under a flexible and tractable methodology.

Table 2.1 summarizes the advantages and drawbacks of these five types of models: nonspatial partial equilibrium, spatial partial equilibrium, single-country general equilibrium, multicountry general equilibrium, and gravity. The usefulness of a methodology is sometimes enhanced through a radical modification; for example, disaggregating households and incorporating household surveys in a single-country general equilibrium model allow worthwhile studies of distributional impacts.

The rest of this study focuses on multicountry general equilibrium models for the following reasons. First, they have been extensively used in recent years to study the potential impact of full trade liberalization or a potential Doha agreement.[6] Second, these studies have drawn a very contradictory picture of these consequences, so that their credibility has been questioned. Third, these models are often treated as "black boxes," the results of which are difficult to understand.

The next chapter focuses on an evaluation of full trade liberalization using the MIRAGE model. It tries to put in perspective the stakes of trade reform for developing countries while highlighting the advantages and drawbacks of the analytical instrument.

---

[6]See, for example, the development of the GTAP network, but also the works of the World Bank (2002, 2004a) and of Cline (2004).

Chapter 3

A New Assessment of the Impact of Trade Liberalization

The objective of this chapter is to carry out an experiment using a multi-country CGEM that analyzes the impact of full trade liberalization on world income and developing countries. World poverty is mainly found in the agricultural sector, which is also subjected to major trade distortions worldwide. Thus, full trade liberalization should entail a positive impact on poverty alleviation. Liberalization of the textile and clothing industry—which is labor intensive—could bolster economic activity and contribute to poverty reduction in developing countries. Moreover, elimination of domestic distortions could enhance welfare and economic growth.

Nevertheless, some questions remain. Some developing countries are highly specialized in products for which distortions are very low worldwide (for example, coffee, cocoa,[1] and copper). Is there any potential positive impact of full trade liberalization on these economies?

Exports of other developing countries, especially LDCs and Sub-Saharan countries, have been granted large trade preferences by rich countries, especially the EU (for example, the "Cotonou" regime and Everything but Arms [EBA]) and the United States (for example, the African Growth Opportunity Act [AGOA] and the U.S. Caribbean Initiative). Naturally, these developing countries will gain no improvement in market access; instead, they could be negatively affected by tougher competition from large agricultural exporters, such as the Cairns group. Eroded trade preferences have been at the heart of the contention since the beginning of the DDA. This issue requires special attention.

---

[1] Tariffs on coffee and cocoa are low on the raw commodities but high on processed products.

Today, most intervention in agriculture contributes to augmented world production and diminished demand, pushing down world prices of agricultural commodities. Therefore, elimination of these distortions should raise world prices. It could have negative effects on net food-importing countries, however, even if the increase in prices contributes to augmented domestic agricultural production.

These questions lend themselves to theoretical modeling. When liberalizing an economy, welfare gains stem from two major sources: allocative efficiency gains and terms-of-trade gains. A country's own trade reform explains the former: by eliminating import tariffs, consumer surplus is increased and productive factors are allocated more efficiently. These gains are obtained regardless of what trade partners are carrying out. They are called "what you do is what you get" (WYDIWYG) gains (Winters 2000). Terms-of-trade gains can be achieved through raising export prices and/or lowering import prices. Improved access to foreign markets contributes to the former. From a mercantilist point of view, the main goal of trade liberalization is achieved through opening foreign markets and raising exports. In contrast, neoclassical theory emphasizes allocative efficiency gains (WYDIWYG gains).

The theoretical basis of CGEM is neoclassical. In this sense, allocative efficiency gains are fundamental in these studies: WYDIWYG gains have even been considered as the major source of gains for developing countries in the Uruguay Round of trade talks. From a policy perspective, it means that every country will gain from its own trade reform.

But CGEMs capture other sources of gain through the evolution of terms of trade (for constant trade volumes, increased export prices or decreased import prices mean improvement in terms of trade, whereas decreased export prices or increased import prices mean deterioration in terms of trade). Terms-of-trade effects might be negative, so that multilateral liberalization can imply welfare losses for a country. From a policy perspective, this loss could be a result of tougher competition on export markets (eroded preferences imply that exports are receiving more competitive pressure)—which entails reduced export prices—or rising import prices.

Thus, in this kind of modeling exercise, methodological choices are fundamental. Aggregating all developing countries in one zone, for example, would mislead policy conclusions: a global zone composed of South America and Sub-Saharan Africa would be a net food-exporting zone, but some Sub-Saharan African countries are net food-importing countries. To tackle the issues previously mentioned, special attention has to be given to the geographic decomposition of the model. Also, the importance of the way in which competition is modeled and dynamic gains are captured should be emphasized. A sensitivity analysis has to be specifically devoted to these issues.

The next three sections describe the technical features of MIRAGE and the geographical and sector decomposition adopted. The fourth section presents the pre-experiment scenario and draws a picture of the world just before implementing full trade liberalization: level of gross domestic product (GDP) and trade, and level of distortions. The final section in the chapter describes the impact of full trade liberalization at both the world and country levels. It finally decomposes the shock (the shock is the trade reform implemented in the model) to tackle the main economic policy issues: which countries are the main beneficiaries? Which are the most distorting measures?

Technical Presentation of MIRAGE

MIRAGE is a multisector, multiregion CGEM devoted to trade policy analysis. The model is done in a sequential dynamic recursive set-up: it is solved for one period, and then all variable values, determined at the end of a period, are used as the initial values of the next one. Macroeconomic data and social accounting matrixes, in particular, come from the GTAP 6 database (see Dimaranan 2006), which describes the world economy in 2001. Tariff averages have been recalculated using the MacMap methodology (see Bouët et al. 2006, 2008).

From the supply side in each sector, the production function is a Leontief function of value-added and intermediate inputs: one output unit needs for its production x percent of an aggregate of productive factors (labor, unskilled and skilled; capital; land and natural resources) and $(1 - x)$ percent of intermediate inputs.[2]

The intermediate inputs function is an aggregate CES function of all goods: it means that substitutability exists between two intermediate goods, depending on the relative prices of these goods. This substitutability is constant and at the same level for any pair of intermediate goods. Similarly, value-added is a CES function of unskilled labor, land, natural resources, and of a CES bundle of skilled labor and capital. This nesting allows the modeler to introduce less substitutability between capital and skilled labor than between these two and other factors. In other words, when the relative price of unskilled labor is increased, this factor is replaced by a combination of capital and skilled labor, which are more complementary.[3]

Factor endowments are fully employed. The only factor whose supply is constant is natural resources. Capital supply is modified each year because of depreciation and investment. Growth rates of labor supply are fixed exogenously. Land supply is endogenous; it depends on the real remuneration of land. In some countries

---

[2]The fixed-proportion assumption for intermediate inputs and primary factor inputs is especially pertinent to developed economies, but for some developing economies that are undergoing dramatic economic growth and structural change, such as China, the substitution between intermediate inputs and primary factor inputs may be significant.

[3]Substitution elasticity between unskilled labor, land, natural resources, and the bundle of capital and skilled labor is 1.1, whereas it is only 0.6 between capital and skilled labor.

land is a scarce factor (for example, Japan and the EU), such that elasticity of supply is low. In others (such as Argentina, Australia, and Brazil), land is abundant and elasticity is high.

Skilled labor is the only factor that is perfectly mobile. Installed capital and natural resources are sector specific. New capital is allocated among sectors according to an investment function. Unskilled labor is imperfectly mobile between agricultural and nonagricultural sectors according to a constant elasticity of transformation (CET) function: unskilled labor's remuneration in agricultural activities is different from that in nonagricultural activities. This factor is distributed between these two series of sectors according to the ratio of remunerations. Land is also imperfectly mobile among agricultural sectors.

Therefore, in MIRAGE there is full employment of labor; more precisely, there is a constant aggregate employment in all countries (wage flexibility). It is quite possible to suppose that total aggregate employment is variable and that there is unemployment; but this choice greatly increases the complexity of the model, so that simplifying assumptions have to be made in other areas (such as the number of countries or sectors). This assumption could amplify the benefits of trade liberalization for developing countries (see Diao et al. 2005): in full-employment models, increased demand for labor (from increased activity and exports) leads to higher real wages, such that the origin of comparative advantage is progressively eroded; but in models with unemployment, real wages are constant and exports increase much more.

Capital in a given region, whatever its origin, domestic or foreign, is assumed to be obtained by assembling intermediate inputs according to a specific combination. The capital good is the same whatever the sector. MIRAGE describes imperfect, as well as perfect, competition. In sectors under perfect competition, there is no fixed cost, and price equals marginal cost. Imperfect competition is modeled according to a monopolistic competition framework. It accounts for horizontal product differentiation linked to product variety. Each firm in sectors under imperfect competition produces its own unique variety, with a fixed cost expressed as a fixed quantity of output. According to the Cournot hypothesis, each firm supposes that its decision of production will not affect the production of other firms. Furthermore, the firms do not expect that their decision of production will affect the level of domestic demand (which would be what modelers call a "Ford effect").

The monopolistic competition framework implies that each year, firms exert their market power by applying a markup to their marginal costs. This markup depends negatively on the price elasticity of demand according to the Lerner formula. This price elasticity, as perceived by firms, depends positively on the elasticity of substitution between the goods produced domestically and abroad, and negatively on the number of competitors and the market share of the firm in the demand region.[4] In the long term, the number of firms is endogenous, as it increases when profits are positive. An implication of this hypothetical structure is that international trade has procompetitive effects and reduces mark-ups and prices.

The number of firms may adjust progressively, either quickly (2 years in fragmented sectors) or slowly (5 years in segmented sectors). This classification is based on the seminal work of Sutton (1991) and has been confirmed by Oliveira-Martins (1994) and Oliveira-Martins, Scarpetta, and Pilat (1996). These works are the basis of the taxonomy used by MIRAGE to distinguish fragmented and segmented sectors.

Thus, the latest version of MIRAGE includes the following assumptions:

- imperfect mobility of labor between agricultural and nonagricultural sectors;
- endogenous land supply; and
- the European land set-aside program (this program decreases the quantity of land available for production in the wheat sector).

The demand side is modeled in each region through a representative agent whose propensity to save is constant. The rest of the national income is used to purchase final consumption. Preferences across sectors are represented by a linear expenditure system–constant elasticity of substitution (LES-CES) function. It implies that consumption has a nonunitary income elasticity; when the consumer's income is augmented by x percent, the consumption of each good is not systematically raised by x percent.

When competition is imperfect, the product is horizontally differentiated (called "product variety"), and consumers have increased utility with more variety; this hypothesis is a traditional one (the Spence-Dixit-Stiglitz function). But MIRAGE introduces here two specific features. First, in some sectors (such as industry), products coming from developed countries and those from developing countries are supposed to belong to different quality ranges. Their substitutability, therefore, is assumed to be lower than the substitutability among products coming from the same quality range. Second, domestic products benefit from a specific status of consumers; they are less substitutable for foreign products than foreign products are among one another within a given quality range.

The sector subutility function used in MIRAGE is a nesting of four CES functions. In this study, Armington elasticities are drawn from the GTAP 5 database and are assumed to be the same across regions. The other elasticities used in the nesting for a given sector are linked to the Armington elasticity by a simple rule (see Bchir

---

[4]This specification is very close to the one used by Harrison, Rutherford, and Tarr (1997).

et al. 2002 for more details). Finally, the elasticity of substitution in the LES-CES function is set at 0.6. Macroeconomic closure is obtained by assuming that the sum of the balance of goods and services and foreign direct investments (FDIs) is constant and equal to its initial value.

Geographic Decomposition

Table 3.1 indicates the geographical decomposition that was designed for this study. Given that the study is an assessment of trade liberalization on developing countries, 14 of the 20 selected zones are developing countries.[5] Table 3.1 reflects specific characteristics of various countries and regions. The reason, for example, that the EU and the United States are presented as separate zones is because they have the richest markets in the world and they have granted large trade preferences. Australia and New Zealand are powerful agricultural exporting countries, which could be among the main beneficiaries of this trade shock. The zone called "Developed Asia" includes countries with extremely high protectionism in agriculture (Japan, South Korea, and Taiwan). In other rich countries, Canada has a very low density of rural population per arable land area. The zone Rest of OECD is composed of rich countries (Mexico is not included) with land as a scarce factor and with a very high protectionism in agriculture: Switzerland, Norway, and Iceland.

As far as developing countries are concerned, India and China have been treated as distinct zones, because between them they include 37 percent of world population and 50 percent of world poverty (using the US$2.00 per day definition).[6] Moreover, these countries could be winners of worldwide full trade liberalization for different reasons:

1. Liberalization would entail eliminating large domestic distortions, as today they are highly protected countries (especially India).[7]
2. These countries have been granted only small trade preferences, such that liberalization should imply a significant improvement of their market access to the rest of the world.

Brazil and Argentina are powerful agricultural exporting countries with very large productive capacities, and they have only been conceded a small preference in their access to Europe and the United States, compared to other developing coun-

---

[5]Table B.1 gives the geographic and sector correspondence table between these decompositions and the GTAP classification.

[6]These data on population and poverty are from the World Bank (2003).

[7]According to the MacMap-HS6 database, the average protection tariff in India was 33.5 percent in 2001. China is less protected, with an average tariff of 14.1 percent in the same year.

Table 3.1   Geographical decomposition

Country/zone	North/South	Is land a scarce factor?
Australia/New Zealand	North	No
Canada	North	No
Developed Asia	North	Yes
European Union 25	North	Yes
United States	North	No
Rest of OECD	North	Yes
Argentina	South	No
Bangladesh	South	Yes
Brazil	South	No
China	South	Yes
Developing Asia	South	Yes
India	South	Yes
Mexico	South	Yes
Southern African Customs Union	South	Yes
Tunisia	South	Yes
Zambia	South	Yes
Rest of Latin America	South	Yes
Rest of Middle East and North Africa	South	Yes
Rest of Sub-Saharan Africa	South	Yes
Rest of the World	South	Yes

Notes: The terminology "North/South" is traditional in international economics and distinguishes between rich (OECD) and poor (non-OECD) countries. OECD, Organisation for Economic Co-operation and Development.

tries. In contrast, Tunisia and Bangladesh could be penalized for two reasons: they are net food-importing countries and their export performance has been bolstered by large trade preferences (the Euromed partnership in the case of Tunisia, EBA in the case of Bangladesh). Zambia mostly exports copper, which is only marginally taxed by import duties throughout the world. Moreover, Zambia is a beneficiary of all main preferential schemes: EBA, AGOA, and the Generalized System of Preferences (GSP). The Southern African Customs Union (SACU) must be distinguished from the rest of Sub-Saharan Africa: its members are not LDCs, except for Lesotho. Mexico has a relatively low average income per capita and free access to the United States. It may also be affected by an erosion of trade preferences.

Finally, four developing zones have been distinguished because of the specificity of their geographic trade composition: the rest of developing Asia, the rest of the Middle East and North Africa, the rest of Latin America (excluding OECD countries) and the rest of Sub-Saharan African countries. The Middle East and North Africa zone is a large net food-importing zone, and it exports mainly primary, non-agricultural, and oil commodities. This product structure of exports is also a feature of the Rest of Latin America zone (Bolivia, Chile, and Venezuela). The rest of Sub-

Saharan countries have extended export preferences for Europe and the United States. Thus, the geographical decomposition of this study emphasizes the heterogeneity of developing countries according to forces that could contribute to improved welfare for some countries (Brazil, China, and India) but also to great losses for others (Bangladesh, Mexico, Tunisia, and Zambia).

Since the launching of the DDA, several negotiating blocks have appeared, adding complexity to this process, compared to the negotiations between the United States and the EU, which characterized the previous trade rounds. The geographical decomposition used here also illustrates the new partition: the United States, the EU, the rich countries of the Cairns group (Australia, Canada, and New Zealand), the G-10 (with the Developed Asia zone and the Rest of OECD zone), the G-20 (Argentina, Brazil, China, India, and South Africa), the G-90 (Zambia, Tunisia, and Rest of Sub-Saharan Africa). Thus, this model could also be utilized to explain the positions of these negotiating blocks.

Product Decomposition

The sector decomposition emphasizes the existence of key sectors in which distortions are high and numerous. Of course, agriculture must be the main focus of study, which is why out of the 17 sectors considered, 9 are agricultural. Among these agricultural activities, some are of key concern, as their distortions are especially high: tariffs for wheat, sugar, meat, rice, and milk; and domestic support for cotton (plant-based fibers). In the case of sugar, rice, and milk, the processed goods have been isolated, because paddy rice, raw milk, sugar cane, and sugar beet are only marginally traded. Finally, vegetables and fruits constitute a key agricultural activity for numerous developing countries. Textile and clothing sectors are still highly protected compared to the rest of industrial activity throughout developed countries.

In Table 3.2, the last three columns give valuable information for MIRAGE. In each sector, competition may be perfect or imperfect. According to the traditional point of view, agricultural sectors and transportation are characterized by perfect competition, whereas other sectors are characterized by imperfect competition. According to Oliveira-Martins and Scarpetta (1999) textiles and wearing apparel are assumed to be fragmented; other sectors under imperfect competition are assumed to be segmented. In the version of MIRAGE utilized for this central experiment, unskilled labor is imperfectly mobile between agricultural and nonagricultural activities. The last column indicates this distinction: here the food sector is considered as agricultural.

First, a pre-experiment is conducted to account for the liberalization that occurred from 2001 to 2005. Then, full trade liberalization is applied by eliminating, in all countries, tariffs, domestic support, and export subsidies linearly in 10 years.

Table 3.2   Sector decomposition

Sector	Type of competition	Segmented/ fragmented	Agricultural/ nonagricultural
Wheat	Perfect	—	Agricultural
Vegetables and fruits	Perfect	—	Agricultural
Plant-based fibers	Perfect	—	Agricultural
Meat: cattle, sheep, goat, horse	Perfect	—	Agricultural
Milk (processed)	Perfect	—	Agricultural
Rice (processed)	Perfect	—	Agricultural
Sugar (processed)	Perfect	—	Agricultural
Other food products	Perfect	—	Agricultural
Other agricultural products	Perfect	—	Agricultural
Other primary products	Perfect	—	Nonagricultural
Textiles	Imperfect	Fragmented	Nonagricultural
Wearing apparel	Imperfect	Fragmented	Nonagricultural
Metal, mineral, petroleum, and chemical products	Imperfect	Segmented	Nonagricultural
Vehicles and equipment	Imperfect	Segmented	Nonagricultural
Other manufacturing products	Imperfect	Segmented	Nonagricultural
Other services	Imperfect	Segmented	Nonagricultural
Transport and trade	Perfect	—	Nonagricultural

Notes: See text for definitions of fragments and segmented; —, not applicable.

The Initial World

The Pre-Experiment

Initial data (the social accounting matrix and tariffs) are from 2001. As substantial liberalization occured between 2001 and 2005, a pre-experiment is conducted: data on market access are changed to include the last implementation of the Uruguay Round, the elimination of the Multi-Fibre Arrangement, enlargement of the EU, implementation of the EBA initiative and the AGOA, and finally, the accession of China to the WTO. These reforms should result in welfare benefits but are not part of a current deal on trade liberalization.

Main Features of the Initial Trading System

The initial world is characterized by a few statistics presented in Tables C.1–C.4 and Figures 3.1–3.5: levels of tariffs, export structure by destination, export structure by product, and net trade balance in agricultural and food products. This choice is justified by the arguments mentioned previously: domestic support and export subsidies are only minor distortions compared to tariffs; preferential access to a large market is a common feature, such that its erosion is a central concern; and agricultural world prices are expected to rise, so that being a net importer or exporter is a key issue.

Table C.1 gives bilateral levels of protection for each zone in 2005. Each row defines the average tariff charged by an importing country (for example, Canada taxes products coming from the Australia/New Zealand zone at 6.7 percent), while each column indicates the average duty faced by a country on its exports to a specific destination. The last column indicates the average protection in each zone (protectionism that a country imposes on its imports), and the last row expresses the average duty faced by exports (the extent to which a country's exports are penalized by foreign protectionism). This information is summarized in Figure 3.1.

India is by far the most protectionist country, but trade barriers are also high in Bangladesh, Sub-Saharan Africa, and Tunisia; they are marginally less so in Brazil, Argentina, and Zambia. Global protection in rich countries is lower. Because of preferential schemes (EBA, AGOA, Cotonou, and Caricom) or specialization in products lightly taxed across the world (coffee, coca, cotton, and mining), numerous developing countries are facing low average tariffs on their exports: Tunisia, Rest of Sub-Saharan Africa, Bangladesh, Zambia, and especially Mexico and Rest of Middle East and North Africa. For Mexico, the North American Free Trade Agree-

Figure 3.1   Protection applied by and faced by zone, 2005

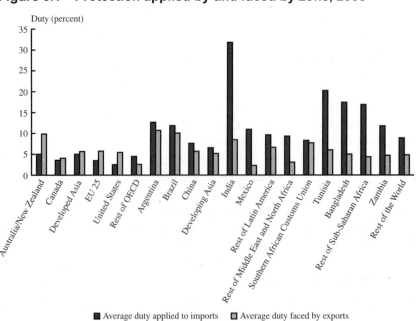

ment (NAFTA) provides free access to a major market, while for the other zones this relief is a combination of two elements—Euromed partnerships and exportation of raw commodities—which explains the very low average duty faced on exports. In the case of Argentina, Australia, Brazil, and New Zealand, specialization in agriculture implies that their exports are penalized more than those of other countries. Conversely, specialization in industry gives relatively good access to foreign markets: Canada, China, Developed Asia, the EU, and the United States.

The necessity of taking fully into account preferential schemes and regional agreements is now widely admitted by the international community of researchers. It has changed the global picture of world protection, not only because average world protection is now considered lower than previously thought (see above), but also because trade policies from industrial countries appear to be less antidevelopment. For example, in 2004 the Global Economic Prospects of the World Bank (2004a, 81) emphasized the regressive aspect of trade policies:

Tariffs imposed by the industrial countries on imports from developing countries are typically much higher than those they levy on other industrial countries. In agriculture, the industrial countries impose an average 15 percent tariff on imports from other industrial countries, whereas the rates on imports from developing countries range from 20 percent (Latin America) to 35 percent (Europe and Central Asia). Outside of agriculture, the discrepancy is even more striking. Tariffs on imports from other industrial countries average 1 percent, while those from developing countries face tariff averages ranging from 2.1 percent (Latin America) to 8.1 percent (south Asia).

From Jean, Laborde, and Martin (2005, 104–105) it now appears that

Developing countries' exporters of agricultural products faced an average tariff of 16 percent in 2001, a rate that is expected to fall to 15 percent once current commitments, particularly by China and other developing countries, are phased in. The average tariff facing industrial countries was 17 percent in 2001, and will fall to 16 percent with full implementation of current commitments. The LDCs as a group face lower, but still significant barriers, with an average tariff of 12 percent even after preferences are taken into account.

In agriculture, the imposition of specific duties by numerous rich countries (Switzerland, the EU, and Norway) has a very negative impact on protection faced by developing countries: because they export products of lower unit value on average, the rate of protection associated with the same duty is higher. Nevertheless, the impact of preferential schemes is substantial. Thus, globally, trade policies are progressive, in the sense that the poorest countries are facing lower average duties on their exports than richer countries face; the policies are not regressive, as previously thought (and stated, for example, in World Bank 2004a). Of course, these two new qualifications (lower world protection and "progressive" trade policies) are key elements to keep in mind when explaining trade pessimism.

In Europe, preferences have been given to Bangladesh and Sub-Saharan Africa (EBA), the Middle East and North Africa (the Euro–Mediterranean partnership), the rest of OECD (the EU–European Free Trade Agreement [EFTA] agreement); in the United States, to Canada and Mexico (NAFTA), and to Sub-Saharan Africa (AGOA). Table C.1 shows that these schemes imply systematically lower rates of protection.

Table C.2 gives the level of protection by importing country and/or zone and product, and Figure 3.2 provides a graphical snapshot of the world average protection by product. Protection is very high in the case of rice (with a record duty of 615 percent in Developed Asia), sugar, and milk; it is also substantial for meat and wheat. In industry, only textiles and wearing apparel are significantly taxed.

Table C.3 provides detailed information, and Figure 3.3 gives a synthetic representation of the initial geographical structure of exports: rich countries and, in particular, Developed Asia, Europe, and the United States are the main destinations of world exports. It also highlights the impact of regional agreements or preferential schemes; trade is highly concentrated in North America (from Canada and Mexico

Figure 3.2   World average import duty, by product, 2005

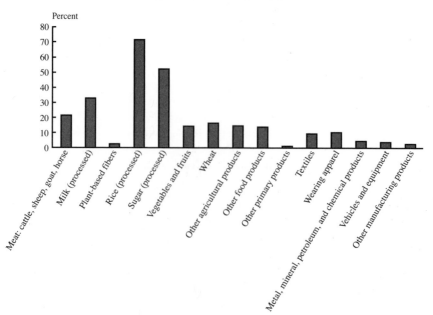

Figure 3.3   Geographical structure of exports, 2005

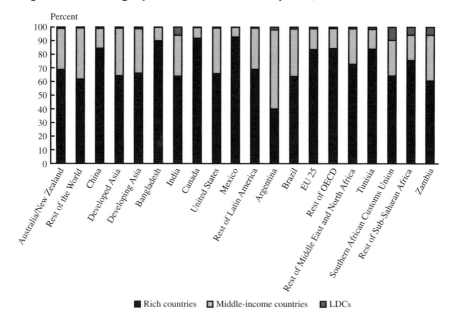

to the United States) and in Europe (inside the EU and from the EFTA–Rest of OECD to the EU). The EU is by far the most likely destination for exports from Tunisia and, to a lesser extent, Sub-Saharan Africa. Figure 3.3 illustrates the global heterogeneity in destinations of exports from developing countries. While Bangladesh, China, Mexico, and Tunisia concentrate their exports on the markets of rich countries, Argentina clearly prioritizes middle-income countries for its exports.

Figure 3.4 illustrates the product composition of exports (detailed information is in Table C.4). Some countries, such as Zambia (for which 70 percent of exports consists of metal, mineral, petroleum, and chemical products) and Bangladesh (for which 70 percent of exports consists of textiles and wearing apparel), are specialized in mining activities and industry; others are specialized in agriculture (Australia/New Zealand, Brazil, and especially Argentina).

Figure 3.5 shows the net trade balance of the 20 zones in agricultural and food products. Such zones as Rest of Middle East and North Africa, Rest of OECD, Developed Asia, EU 25, and Mexico are net food importers and could lose from an increase in agricultural world prices. Conversely, Argentina, Australia/New Zealand, Brazil, and the United States are large net food exporters.

It is noteworthy that no simple categorization of developing countries as net food exporters and developed countries as net food importers can be made:

Figure 3.4   Product composition of exports, 2005

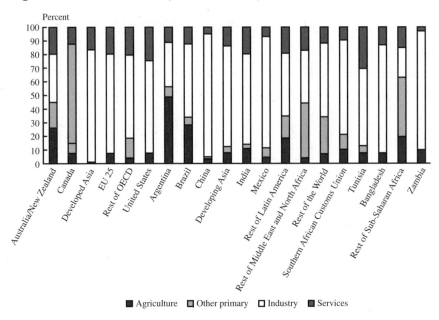

Figure 3.5   Net exports of agricultural and food products, 2005

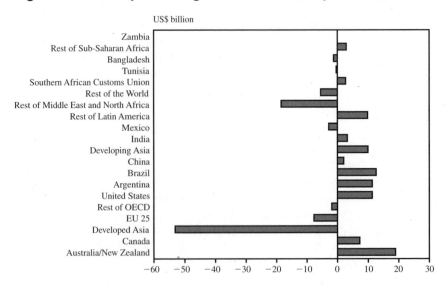

Australia/New Zealand is the largest net exporter of food, whereas some developing zones are net food importers. Similarly, preferential margins have been granted to LDCs and developed countries (Canada, Mexico, and the EFTA).

Expected Benefits from Trade Liberalization

Before describing the results of the impact at the country level, I analyze the impact of full trade liberalization at the world level.

Impact of Full Liberalization at the World Level

Compared to the baseline situation, full trade liberalization increases world welfare (real income) by 0.33 percent, or US$99.6 billion (Table 3.3).[8] When focusing on the rate of increase in real income, if the reference is the last group of assessments based on recent data on market access and domestic support, this result is close to those of Hertel and Keeney (2005) and Francois, Van Meijl, and Van Tongeren (2005). But it is smaller than the results of Anderson, Martin, and Van der Mensbrugghe (2005a). The difference between the values given in Table 3.3 and Cline's results (2004) is large, as it is with the assessments of the World Bank (2002, 2004a). This welfare increase is associated with an augmentation of world trade by 5.25 percent. Because trade barriers are numerous in the agricultural sector, world agricultural trade increases by 6.5 times more: 33.67 percent.

Trade liberalization consists of eliminating import tariffs and production and export subsidies. Thus, it increases world demand and decreases world supply, contributing to an augmentation of world prices. This point is confirmed by Figure 3.6, which indicates the evolution of world prices after trade liberalization (see also the first column of Table D.1 in Appendix D) for all sectors. But price augmentations are uneven: although they are only minor in industry and services, they are large in agriculture, especially for wheat, plant-based fibers, and other agricultural products. These increases in agricultural world prices are quite similar to those obtained by other studies (see, for example, Diao, Somwaru, and Roe 2001).

Table D.1 indicates the evolution of world prices by exporting countries. In a model like MIRAGE, there is no single world price for a specific commodity: according to the Armington (1969) hypothesis, every country produces a specific product; the world price indicated in Figure 3.6 is an average of trade-weighted export prices. The evolution of export prices is particularly divergent among countries for meat, plant-based fibers, (processed) rice, (processed) sugar, and wheat.

---

[8]This version of MIRAGE does not include exogenous change in total factor productivity, which is accounted for in such models as LINKAGE (a global dynamic CGEM maintained by the World Bank to support global trade policy analysis; see Van der Mensbrugghe 2005). As a consequence, it is better to make comparisons on a relative basis.

Table 3.3   Impact of full trade liberalization: Rate of change for world indicators for 2015 (percent)

Indicator	Total
World agricultural trade	33.67
World merchandise trade	5.25
World welfare	0.33

Figure 3.6   Impact of full trade liberalization: Rate of change of world prices for 2015 compared to baseline

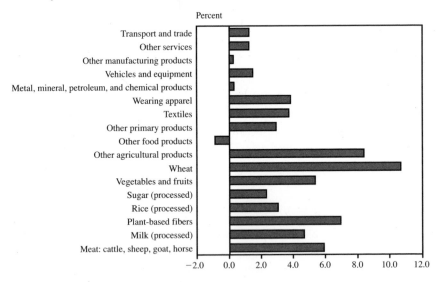

Impact of Full Liberalization at the Country Level

What is the impact of this trade reform for different countries in the model? It is progressive: the increase in welfare is proportionally higher for developing countries, especially for LDCs (see Table 3.4), although their share of the overall world welfare increase is smaller. The rate of change in welfare is two times greater for LDCs than for middle-income countries and more than two times greater than for rich countries. In this sense, full liberalization is development friendly.

This result does not mean, however, that each developing country profits evenly from this higher rate of change in welfare. Table 3.5 shows that welfare gains are unequally distributed among developing countries. In this table, countries are ranked by income levels: first, the rich countries, then the middle-income countries, and finally the LDCs. This information is completed by macroeconomic indicators on production and exports in Table 3.6.

There are several sources of variation in welfare gains. First, distortions are reduced, and productive factors are reallocated to sectors where they are more efficient. Table 3.5 indicates these gains in allocation efficiencies, which are systemati-

Table 3.4   Distribution of welfare gains among beneficiary groups and rate of change in welfare (percent)

Beneficiary group	Share of total welfare gain	Increase in welfare
Rich countries	73.8	0.3
Middle-income countries	24.1	0.4
Least-developed countries	2.2	0.8

Note: The numbers in column "Share of total welfare gain" add up to slightly more than 100 percent because of roundoff errors.

Table 3.5   Impact of full trade liberalization: Rate of change in macroeconomic indicators for 2015 (percent)

Country/zone	Welfare	Allocation efficiency gains	Terms-of-trade gains
Australia/New Zealand	0.9	0.1	1.4
Canada	−0.1	0.6	0.2
Developed Asia	1.4	2.3	0.1
EU 25	−0.1	0.2	−0.1
Rest of OECD	1.0	1.0	0.1
United States	0.1	0.0	0.1
Argentina	−0.1	0.3	0.3
Brazil	0.2	0.1	0.4
China	0.6	0.8	0.1
Developing Asia	0.4	0.7	−0.1
India	0.7	1.5	−0.9
Mexico	−0.3	1.3	−0.5
Rest of Latin America	0.0	0.8	−0.2
Rest of Middle East and North Africa	0.9	1.2	−0.5
Rest of the World	0.1	0.9	0.0
Southern African Customs Union	−0.2	0.3	0.6
Tunisia	0.4	0.4	−0.4
Bangladesh	1.5	1.8	−1.1
Rest of Sub-Saharan Africa	0.6	1.3	−0.6
Zambia	0.3	1.6	−2.4

Note: OECD, Organisation for Economic Co-operation and Development.

Table 3.6   Full trade liberalization: Rate of change of macroeconomic indicators for production and exports (percent by volume)

Country/zone	Agrifood production	Nonagrifood production	Exports
Australia/New Zealand	18.3	−1.5	10.1
Canada	−2.8	−0.1	−3.7
Developed Asia	−6.4	−0.2	6.8
EU 25	−2.5	−0.2	−4.4
Rest of OECD	−10.8	0.2	0.8
United States	0.5	−0.2	−0.5
Argentina	7.5	−2.5	12.5
Brazil	12.2	−1.3	21.7
China	−0.2	0.8	9.0
Developing Asia	7.1	0.3	8.8
India	−4.0	2.8	52.2
Mexico	−4.9	−1.8	4.4
Rest of Latin America	4.4	−1.2	20.0
Rest of Middle East and North Africa	−6.1	1.6	11.9
Rest of the World	−3.4	−1.4	14.3
Southern African Customs Union	7.6	−1.4	6.4
Tunisia	0.8	1.1	−4.2
Bangladesh	0.7	2.7	55.5
Rest of Sub-Saharan Africa	−4.0	−0.4	19.2
Zambia	−4.4	3.2	21.2

Note: OECD, Organisation for Economic Co-operation and Development.

cally positive, as numerous distortions are eliminated.[9] Second, terms of trade are modified. A better access to foreign markets increases export prices, while, on the contrary, erosion of preferences implies more competition in export markets and lower export prices. Furthermore, because distortions are numerous in agricultural sectors, full trade liberalization entails an increase in the relative world price of these commodities. Agricultural exporters are generally benefiting from an improvement in their terms of trade, whereas net food-importing countries are penalized.

Nevertheless, consideration of only the initial agrifood balance can be misleading: trade of wheat, sugar, rice, and meat is severely distorted, whereas other agricultural products are much less distorted. Specialization of each country is not evenly distributed in all agricultural sectors. For example, agricultural exports of India, Rest

---

[9]Because some distortions, such as (final and intermediate) consumption taxes, remain after the shock, and because the economic variable on which these taxes are levied can be modified by trade reform, allocation efficiency losses could occur.

of Latin America, and Developing Asia are highly concentrated in the category of other food products (at a level of 46, 45, and 61 percent, respectively). This is the only agrifood commodity for which the world price decreases after trade reform (see Figure 3.6). Conversely, these three zones are also net exporters of industrial products whose world prices remain almost constant (metal, mineral, petroleum, and chemical products). As a result, these three zones lose from a deterioration of their terms of trade, even if they were initially net food-exporting countries (Table 3.5).

But like other models of its generation, MIRAGE captures other effects of welfare changes (otherwise the first column in Table 3.5 would be equal to the sum of the two other columns—which is why, in the case of Argentina, Canada, and Southern African Customs Union, total gains coming from allocative efficiency and terms of trade are very different from welfare gains). It accounts for imperfect competition activities, so that expansion of these sectors implies new welfare effects. As production increases, average costs and prices are cut, which results in greater efficiency. Moreover, as horizontal differentiation is modeled, selling on a larger scale allows for an increased product variety to be produced: it implies accrued utility for consumers who value variety.

Conversely, as already noted by Francois, Van Meijl, and Van Tongeren (2005), this feature has negative consequences on countries where specialization in perfect-competition activities (agriculture) increases because of liberalization. Compared to the baseline, it might entail a smaller economic activity in industry, fewer economies of scale, and less product variety.

Finally, in MIRAGE, as in the World Bank's LINKAGE model, land supply is endogenous and is determined by real remuneration of this productive factor. The elasticity of land supply is higher in zones (Argentina, Australia/New Zealand, Canada, and the United States) with lower densities of farmers per arable land area.

In rich countries, the impact of full liberalization is positive, except in the case of Europe and Canada, even if this welfare loss is marginal. The welfare gain is quite marginal for the United States, but it is significant for others, because distortions are very high in the case of Developed Asia (Japan, South Korea, and Taiwan), and Rest of OECD (Switzerland, Norway, and Iceland). For Australia/New Zealand, full liberalization implies a significant increase in real exports and activities and a substantial improvement in terms of trade, because it raises the prices of exported goods and provides better access to large markets, such as Europe and the United States. Agrifood production increases by nearly 20 percent in this zone, while it decreases in other rich countries (except the United States, for which the augmentation is insignificant—see Table 3.6).

Agricultural specialization has a mixed effect in the case of Argentina, Australia/New Zealand, and Brazil, as it entails augmented real remuneration and supply of land but less activity in industry and fewer welfare effects associated with this sector.

Agrifood production decreases significantly for Canada, although initially it was a net food exporter. For Canada, multilateral liberalization implies much more severe competition for its primary export destination: the United States (initially 75 percent of its exports). Its export of meat to the United States decreases by 10 percent; vegetables and fruits by 4 percent; rice by 18 percent; clothing and wearing apparel by 28 percent; and metal, mineral, and chemical products, vehicles, and equipment by 9 percent. Globally, this full trade liberalization entails a cut in its total exports of merchandise by nearly 4 percent, resulting from the loss of preferential access to its rich neighbor and reduced activity in both industry and agriculture. This evolution has two negative consequences for Canada: first, industrial activity is reduced compared to the baseline situation; it decreases welfare gains coming from economies of scale and product variety. Second, because agricultural production is negatively affected, real remuneration of land decreases, such that land supply is reduced.

In developing countries, efficiency gains are large where distortions are initially high: Bangladesh, India, and Sub-Saharan Africa. Because Argentina, Brazil, and SACU are large net food exporters, the rise in agricultural world prices implies an improvement in their terms of trade. The zone Rest of Sub-Saharan Africa is initially a net food exporter (see Figure 3.5). Nevertheless, its terms of trade are worsened, because it faces more competition in large markets, such as the EU, where its preferential access is eroded, so its export prices decrease. Furthermore, in the cases of Bangladesh and Rest of Middle East and North Africa, preferences are eroded and prices of imported goods are raised: these two negative effects are cumulative.

The adverse effect of agricultural specialization on welfare gains, which comes from economies of scale and product differentiation, explains global welfare losses of Argentina, Canada, and SACU.[10] Allocating more productive factors to sectors under perfect competition reduces the gain from multilateral liberalization in the case of Australia/New Zealand, Brazil, and Rest of Latin America. Conversely, full trade liberalization expands the industrial sector and increases associated welfare gains in Bangladesh, Tunisia, and Zambia.

The case of Bangladesh is fascinating, as full trade liberalization entails a 55 percent increase in total merchandise exports (by volume). Bangladesh is a highly specialized country, with two sectors (textiles and wearing apparel) representing 70 percent of its exports (see Table C.4). Furthermore, it has a duty-free access to Europe, but its exports to Argentina, Australia/New Zealand, Brazil, Canada, Mexico, and the United States are still highly taxed. This structure of protection and specialization explains such an increase in export performance, but at the same

---

[10]This point is confirmed later by a sensitivity analysis. If the same model is implemented using perfect competition in all sectors, Argentina, for example, experiences a large increase in welfare.

time, trade reform has two negative consequences for this country: first, it faces an increased competition on its exports to Europe (44 percent of total exports), which, in turn, decreases the prices of these exports; second, it is a net food-importing country, and its import prices are raised.

Table 3.7 presents estimates of the impact of full trade liberalization on factor remunerations in real terms. As demonstrated by international trade theory, trade openness has more effect on the real remuneration of less mobile factors. Moreover, because distortions are initially concentrated in the agricultural sector, full trade liberalization has a prominent impact on world prices and activities in this sector. This effect explains why, on one hand, the remuneration of land and natural resources is significantly modified by full trade liberalization, while, on the other hand, capital and skilled labor are much less affected. The real remuneration of land is much reduced by liberalization in Rest of OECD, EU 25, and Developed Asia.[11] This table shows that gains from liberalization have to be shared among several productive factors, whereas losses are concentrated on one or two factors, which may imply strong resistance and weak support for liberalization.

What is the potential impact of trade liberalization on poverty? It cannot be measured in this version of MIRAGE.[12] Nevertheless, Table 3.7 can give some insights into this potential effect. In developing countries, poor people are mostly endowed with unskilled labor. Thus, Table 3.7 points out that full trade liberalization could have a very positive impact on poverty in Bangladesh, Developing Asia, Rest of Sub-Saharan Africa, SACU, Latin America, and Tunisia. It clearly has a contrasting effect on industrial and/or agricultural unskilled labor's wages in China, India, Mexico, and Rest of Middle East and North Africa, where it increases remuneration of unskilled industrial workers and decreases that of agricultural workers. Finally, it has an unambiguously negative effect on low-skilled labor in Zambia.

Trade Liberalization and World Income Distribution

The potential impact of full trade liberalization on world inequality can also be measured. Recent studies (Bourguignon, Levin, and Rosenblatt 2004; Milanovic 2005) focus on comparison of GDP per capita and conclude that world inequality decreased during the 1990s because of rapid growth in China and India.[13] A similar assessment might be done here, but in a prospective way. Although some countries are aggregated into a single set, this calculation gives some insights on the size and the direction of the redistribution associated with trade reform.

---

[11]These three zones were the main contenders for agricultural liberalization during the negotiation of the DDA.

[12]It cannot be measured because poverty elasticities are not used. I explain why later.

[13]Note the exceptional work by Milanovic (2005), who takes into account domestic distribution of income with the use of household surveys; his conclusions are less clear-cut.

Table 3.7   Impact of full trade liberalization: Rate of change of remuneration of production factors for 2015 in real terms (percent)

Country/zone	Agriculture: Unskilled real wages	Industry: Unskilled real wages	Real return to capital	Real return to land	Real return to natural resources	Skilled real wages
Australia/New Zealand	10.3	2.1	–0.7	3.9	–4.4	1.2
Canada	–0.3	–0.3	–0.4	–24.2	4.0	–0.2
Developed Asia	–2.7	1.9	1.4	–30.9	–6.0	2.3
EU 25	0.1	0.3	–0.8	–41.6	–3.8	–0.1
Rest of OECD	–4.9	0.9	1.0	–50.1	5.5	1.2
United States	0.8	0.1	–0.3	–17.0	2.3	0.0
Argentina	5.8	1.5	–1.4	3.0	–6.1	–1.4
Brazil	7.1	1.6	–0.8	4.8	–6.9	0.3
China	–0.7	2.3	–1.7	–7.3	–18.7	4.3
Developing Asia	0.8	1.2	–0.4	–5.3	–16.2	0.9
India	–1.6	1.8	0.1	–4.7	–25.5	4.2
Mexico	–4.4	0.3	0.4	–23.1	–23.1	–2.0
Rest of Latin America	4.2	1.4	–1.1	7.3	–14.2	0.0
Rest of Middle East and North Africa	–2.3	1.0	1.2	–7.4	–11.2	1.3
Rest of the World	–1.1	2.1	–2.3	–5.7	12.4	0.0
Southern African Customs Union	4.8	0.8	–1.7	12.7	8.8	–0.3
Tunisia	1.0	1.1	0.6	–1.0	–7.5	0.3
Bangladesh	1.5	1.3	1.0	1.9	–6.5	0.6
Rest of Sub-Saharan Africa	0.3	1.6	–0.8	–0.4	–4.5	1.5
Zambia	–4.1	–1.0	1.8	–9.0	–22.7	0.6

Note: OECD, Organisation for Economic Co-operation and Development.

Does full trade liberalization reduce world inequality? The answer is that is has no impact, as shown in Table 3.8.[14] Using results on real income from the above modeling exercise, it is possible to calculate real income per capita, with and without full trade liberalization: in Table 3.8, countries are ranked in increasing order according to their real income per capita. Lorenz curves can be constructed using cumulative population (percent) and cumulative real income (percent). Full trade liberalization implies only a very slight move of the Lorenz curve, so that only one curve for the two income distributions appears in Figure 3.7.

Full trade liberalization entails a slight upward move of the Lorenz curve except at four points: those for Argentina, Canada, the EU, and Mexico. The Gini coefficient is reduced from 0.73993 to 0.73981. Globally, free trade means less inequality among countries in the world (with the above limitations), but the impact is

---

[14]Data on expected population levels in 2015 come from the World Bank (2004b).

Table 3.8   World redistribution associated with full trade liberalization

Country/zone	Population (million)	Share of world population (percent)	Cumulative population (percent)	Without full trade liberalization				With full trade liberalization			
				Real income (US$ billion)	Real income per capita (US$ thousand)	Share of world real income (percent)	Cumulative real income (percent)	Real income (US$ billion)	Real income per capita (US$ thousand)	Share of world real income (percent)	Cumulative real income (percent)
Rest of Sub-Saharan Africa	815.8	11.5	11.5	220.05	0.269735229	0.722	0.722	221.413	0.271405982	0.724	0.724
Zambia	11.9	0.2	11.7	3.731	0.313529412	0.012	0.734	3.743	0.314537815	0.012	0.736
Bangladesh	166	2.3	14.0	53.432	0.321879518	0.175	0.910	54.242	0.326759036	0.177	0.914
India	1,231.6	17.4	31.4	563.647	0.457654271	1.850	2.759	567.328	0.460643066	1.856	2.769
Rest of the World	840.65	11.9	43.2	494.929	0.588745614	1.624	4.383	495.592	0.589534289	1.621	4.390
China	1,389.5	19.6	62.8	1145.103	0.824111551	3.758	8.141	1,152.263	0.829264484	3.769	8.159
Developing Asia	728.9	10.3	73.1	787.877	1.080912334	2.585	10.726	791.194	1.085463026	2.588	10.747
Tunisia	11.5	0.2	73.3	19.391	1.686173913	0.064	10.790	19.46	1.692173913	0.064	10.810
Southern African Customs Union	54.4	0.8	74.0	111.224	2.044558824	0.365	11.155	110.997	2.040386029	0.363	11.173
Brazil	201	2.8	76.9	559.103	2.781606965	1.835	12.989	560.388	2.788	1.833	13.006
Rest of Latin America	254.9	3.6	80.5	721.627	2.831020008	2.368	15.357	721.97	2.832365634	2.361	15.368
Mexico	120.6	1.7	82.2	653	5.414593698	2.143	17.500	650.889	5.397089552	2.129	17.497
Argentina	42.9	0.6	82.8	290.751	6.777412587	0.954	18.454	290.374	6.768624709	0.950	18.446
Rest of Middle East and North Africa	162.2	2.3	85.1	1,116.153	6.881337855	3.663	22.117	1,126.301	6.943902589	3.684	22.130
Australia/New Zealand	26.1	0.4	85.4	383.195	14.68180077	1.257	23.374	386.78	14.81915709	1.265	23.395
EU 25	463.2	6.5	92.0	7,724.054	16.67541883	25.346	48.720	7,713.922	16.65354491	25.230	48.625
Canada	33.5	0.5	92.4	644.39	19.23552239	2.114	50.834	643.991	19.22361194	2.106	50.731
Developed Asia	203.6	2.9	95.3	4,278.685	21.01515226	14.040	64.874	4,340.462	21.31857564	14.196	64.928
Rest of OECD	12.55	0.2	95.5	367.598	29.29067729	1.206	66.080	371.353	29.5898048	1.215	66.142
United States	319.9	4.5	100.0	10,337.052	32.31338543	33.920	100.000	10,351.896	32.3597743	33.858	100.000

Note: OECD, Organisation for Economic Co-operation and Development.

Figure 3.7   Lorenz curve on world inequality

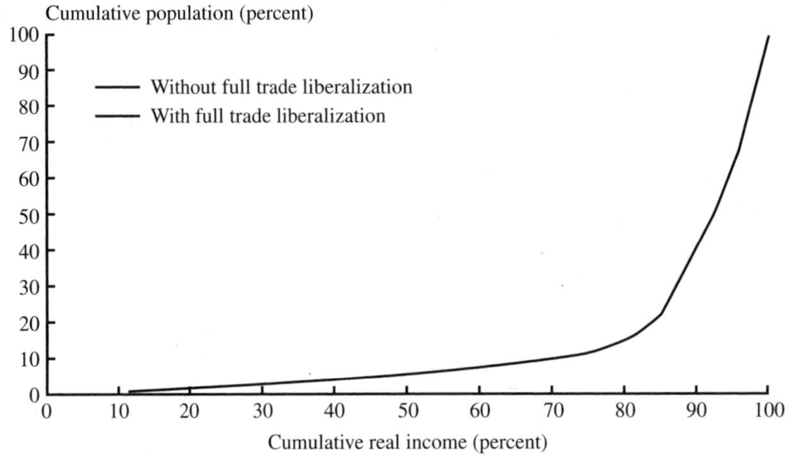

Cumulative population (percent)

— Without full trade liberalization
— With full trade liberalization

Cumulative real income (percent)

minor: this trade reform does not change the fact that 63 percent of world population receives only 8 percent of world income.

This trade reform implies a redistribution of world agricultural production. The United States, Brazil, Australia/New Zealand, Rest of Latin America, Developing Asia, Argentina, China, and SACU increase their net trade balance in these commodities (see Figure 3.8), while the trade deficit in agricultural and food products of Developed Asia, the EU, Rest of Middle East and North Africa, India, and Rest of OECD worsens.

Decomposing Trade Reform

Breaking down trade reform by sources allows for a better understanding of the underlying mechanisms. I study the implementation of successive solitary shocks:[15]

- full trade liberalization in the North, then in the South;
- agricultural liberalization, then industrial liberalization; and
- elimination of import tariffs, then of domestic support, then of export subsidies.

In doing so, the conclusions that emerge from the literature are confirmed. First, developing countries' own trade reforms matter a lot; second, agriculture provides the greatest welfare gains; third, tariffs are by far the main source of distortions.

In the next sections, full trade reform is decomposed successively by liberalizing region (North and South), then by liberalized activity (agriculture and industry),

---

[15]The decomposition technique that is usually adopted (see Harrison, Horridge, and Pearson 2000) is not used here, however, as trade shocks are not considered to be additive.

Figure 3.8   Impact of full trade liberalization on net agricultural exports

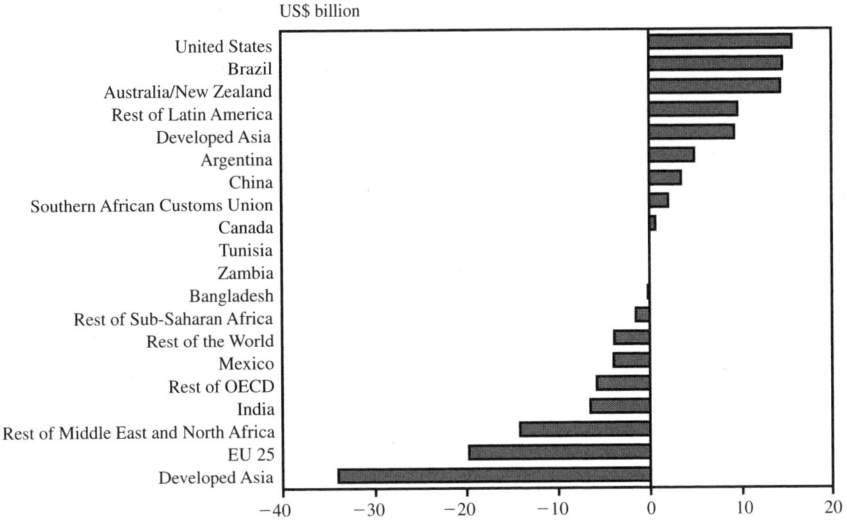

US$ billion

and finally by instrument (tariffs, domestic support, and export subsidies). Detailed results are provided in Appendixes E–G.

Decomposition by liberalizing region.   Figure 3.9 represents welfare gains by country coming from full trade liberalization in the North, and it decomposes such gains into efficiency and terms-of-trade gains. Figure 3.10 provides the same data in the case of full trade liberalization in the South. Liberalization in the North implies the greatest welfare gain (+0.11 percent; see Appendix E), but trade reform in developing countries also matters (+0.06 percent). Although the average protection is higher in the South, dispersion of protection across sectors is higher in rich countries: in that sense, it is more distorting than in the South. Furthermore, liberalizing access in developed countries creates more trade, as these countries are richer.

The origins of these welfare gains are quite different. Efficiency gains are high for the countries that carry out the reform. In the case of Northern liberalization (see Figure 3.9) efficiency gains are large for developed countries and small for developing countries; the opposite is true when liberalization takes place in the South.[16] Terms-of-trade gains are generally positive for developing countries when

---

[16]Exceptions stem from variations in fiscal base while tax and/or subsidy rates are unchanged. For example, if import duties are unchanged but imports increased, efficiency losses are augmented. In Figure 3.9, China is affected by a substantial efficiency loss when liberalization takes place only in the

Figure 3.9   Welfare gains by region: Northern full trade liberalization

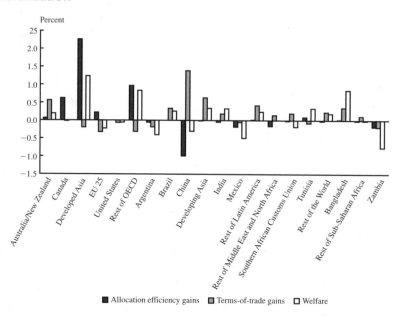

Figure 3.10   Welfare gains by region: Southern full trade liberalization

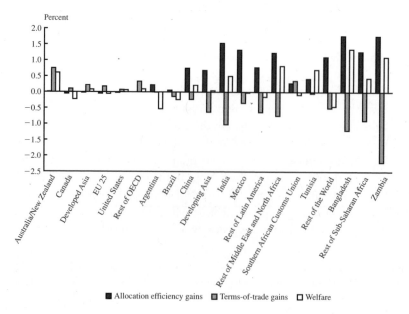

developed countries carry out trade liberalization. This trend stems from the positive impact that the Northern trade reform has on improved market access and on world prices of agricultural goods and textiles/clothing, goods in which developing countries have a comparative advantage.

The exceptions to this scheme are Tunisia and Mexico, whose preferential access to the EU and the United States, respectively, is eroded by multilateral liberalization: more competition in the destination of their exports means reduced export prices. The benefits from Northern liberalization for Argentinean exports are mitigated by an initial geographic concentration on middle-income countries (see Figure 3.3).

The cases of Zambia and Rest of Middle East and North Africa are of great interest, because Northern liberalization for these two zones has negative consequences in terms of real income. Their exports do not profit from improvement of terms of trade or market access, because they either export mainly untaxed products (oil, petroleum, and copper) or their preferential access is eroded. Furthermore, they lose from rising world agricultural prices. On the contrary, reforming their own trade policies brings these two countries significant allocative efficiency gains (see Figure 3.10) and reinforces South–South trade.

On average, terms of trade for developing countries worsen when these countries carry out their own trade reform, although this deterioration is marginal in most cases. For specific countries, the extent to which their terms of trade deteriorate might be large (see India, Bangladesh, and Zambia).

In a nutshell, in general trade reforms in both the North and South matter for developing countries. However, on average Northern trade reform implies improvement of foreign market access and increased export prices, whereas Southern trade reform is beneficial because it entails a reallocation of productive factors to competitive sectors. Nevertheless, Northern trade liberalization can generate welfare losses for developing countries stemming from deterioration of terms of trade.

Decomposition by liberalized activity.   Consider two case scenarios: (1) only agriculture is fully liberalized (see Figure 3.11), and (2) only trade in industry is freed (see Figure 3.12). Agriculture is by far the main source of welfare gains: +0.18 percent (see Appendix F), whereas industrial liberalization entails a minor increase in world welfare. This asymmetry reflects the concentration of distortions in agriculture. On average, world protection is 19.1 percent; it is only 4.2 percent in industry but 10.5 percent in textiles and wearing apparel (these figures are from Bouët et al. 2008). Furthermore, domestic support and export subsidies are concentrated in the agricultural sector, whereas they are rare in industry.

North. The loss comes from high taxes, especially on production, implemented in China. As Northern trade liberalization entails variation in Chinese production, it causes efficiency losses, even if Chinese policies are not modified.

Figure 3.11   Welfare gains by region: Full trade liberalization in agriculture

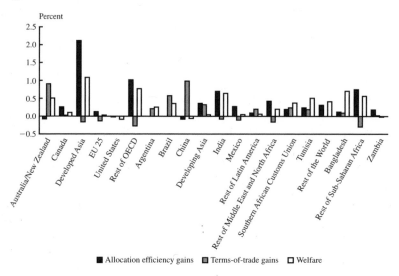

Figure 3.12   Welfare gains by region: Full trade liberalization in industry

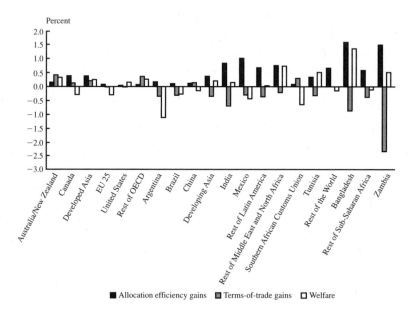

In the same vein, from Figures 3.11 and 3.12, it clearly appears that the level of efficiency gains reflects the initial pattern of protection. In the case of full agricultural liberalization, they are high in Developed Asia, India, Rest of Middle East and North Africa, Rest of OECD, and Rest of Sub-Saharan Africa. For industrial liberalization, efficiency gains are large in Bangladesh, India, Mexico, Rest of Middle East and North Africa, Rest of Sub-Saharan Africa, and Zambia—that is to say, in zones where protection is initially high.

As far as terms-of-trade gains are concerned, as already explained, agricultural liberalization entails a substantial rise in world prices of agricultural commodities. It is beneficial for countries that were initially net exporters of agricultural and food products. Others lose from augmented world agricultural prices, while Mexico and Rest of Sub-Saharan Africa cope with more competition for their main export destinations, for which they lose preferential access.

Argentina, Brazil, Mexico, and Rest of Sub-Saharan Africa have contrasting interests in full trade liberalization, as they gain from agricultural liberalization but lose from industrial liberalization. In the case of Argentina, liberalization of only the industrial sector increases the relative prices of industrial goods, which implies deterioration of terms of trade. Furthermore, industrial sectors attract productive factors, and the remuneration of land is reduced. The land supply decreases, damaging the agrifood sector, which is a prominent sector in the economy. Thus, agricultural reform is a key issue for Argentina.

Except for China and Zambia (which are negatively affected, albeit marginally so), the welfare of developing countries increases with agricultural full trade liberalization, whereas liberalized trade in industry has much more diverse effects.

Decomposition by instrument of intervention.   It is important to note the impact of each distorting instrument. Figures 3.13, 3.14, and 3.15 indicate the impact of fully eliminating border protection, export subsidies, and domestic support, respectively. These three figures have been constructed to the same scale to allow direct comparisons.

Tariffs are by far the main source of distortions. Complete elimination of this instrument increases world welfare by 0.23 percent (see Appendix G). Elimination of domestic support and export subsidies has a small negative effect on world welfare. This conclusion is quite similar to the issue raised by Panagarya (2005). Elimination of domestic support and export subsidies raises world prices of food and affects negatively net food-importing countries, which represent the large majority of low-income countries: Panagarya (2005) concludes that as many as 48 out of 63 low-income countries are net food importers. Even if the removal of these distortions increases the welfare of countries where they are applied (this effect is minor, because price elasticities of agricultural supplies are small) and in food-exporting

Figure 3.13   Welfare gains by region: Full elimination of border protection

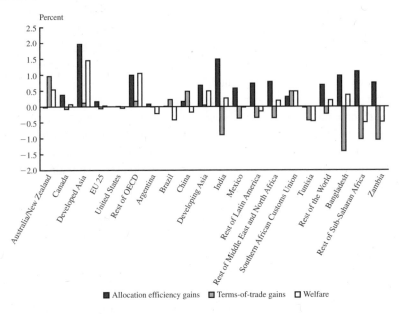

Figure 3.14   Welfare gains by region: Full elimination of export subsidies

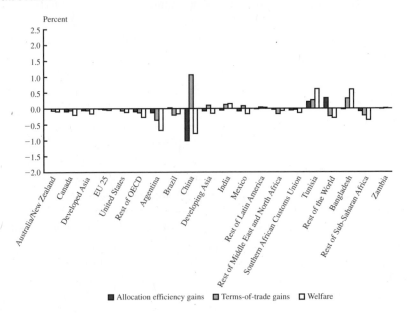

Figure 3.15   Welfare gains by region: Full elimination of domestic support

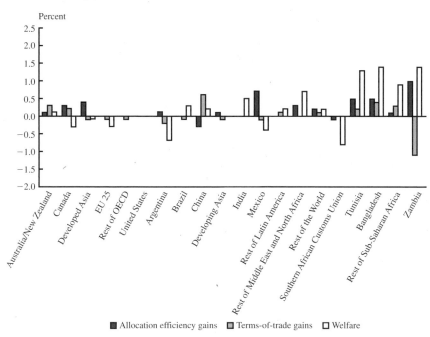

Allocation efficiency gains   Terms-of-trade gains   ☐ Welfare

developing countries (such as Argentina and Brazil), it reduces welfare more substantially in these low-income net food importers. Thus, elimination of domestic support and export subsidies is not a first best policy, and at any rate its global effects may be minor.

Exports subsidies are initially substantial for milk in the EU, Rest of OECD, and the United States; for rice, sugar, and meat in the EU; and for vegetables and fruit in Rest of OECD. In industry, export subsidies are only significant in Rest of Latin America, whereas for the textiles and wearing apparel industries, they are significant in SACU.

Eliminating tariffs creates positive efficiency gains in countries where protection is initially high (Bangladesh, India, and Rest of Sub-Saharan Africa) or exhibits peaks (Developed Asia and Rest of OECD). Tariff is a discriminatory instrument: its elimination has positive effects on terms of trade in Argentina, Brazil, Australia/ New Zealand, and SACU, whereas it entails loss of preferential access for Mexico, Rest of Sub-Saharan Africa, and Zambia. In rich countries, domestic support is high for plant-based fibers, wheat, and other agricultural products. The elimination of this support causes a large increase in world prices of these commodities, which is quite beneficial to their main exporters (Rest of Sub-Saharan Africa).

In conclusion, full trade liberalization improves welfare and promotes development, because welfare enhancements are greater for developing than for developed countries, especially for LDCs. Nevertheless, some topics require further consideration:

- Full liberalization can have adverse effects on individual countries because of terms-of-trade losses; either they are net food-importing countries, so that increased agricultural prices cut their real incomes or they have preferential access, which is eroded by multilateral liberalization. Furthermore, trade liberalization does not significantly improve access to foreign markets in the case of countries that export mainly oil, petroleum, and mineral products.
- Results from the simulation raise a supplementary question: is specialization in agricultural activities a good strategy for development? The simulation indicates that stimulating agricultural specialization entails a smaller expansion of industrial activity, that is to say, fewer economies of scale and less product variety. This conclusion has already been emphasized in the literature (Francois, Van Meijl, and Van Tongeren 2005) and has not been discussed at the political level.

This study might slightly underestimate expected benefits, for at least three reasons. First, the study is based on a database on market access that fully incorporates regional agreements and preferential schemes. Implicitly, full utilization of this preferential access is supposed. Even if this methodology is better than no inclusion of preferences, it has been demonstrated that these preferences are not fully utilized. Thus, the expected benefits for countries receiving preferences, which are mostly developing countries, are underestimated.

Second, the simulation is based on low trade elasticities. This choice can be justified. Recent econometric work by Hertel et al. (2000) gives a scientific basis for using these behavioral parameters. This element is primordial (the welfare effect is directly related to trade creation, which depends on the level of trade elasticities) and has to be kept in mind.

Third, the study's estimation is founded on decomposition into 17 sectors and 20 geographic zones. This choice is quite representative compared to the literature and is also justified by the theoretical features. The model accounts for imperfect competition, horizontal and vertical differentiation, and imperfect mobility of unskilled labor between agricultural and nonagricultural activities. It is also dynamic. Thus, increasing the number of products and regions would have also augmented the number of equations and the calculation time. But a less detailed product and geographic decomposition inevitably underestimates the distortions created by protection, because tariffs are unevenly distributed across products and regions.

A 0.33 percent increase in real income represents a modest contribution to economic growth—surprisingly low when the East Asian miracle is considered, for example. Four reasons may contribute to this low result. First, trade liberalization is not the only factor of economic growth, and domestic reform may have a huge impact on economic performance. Second, the experiment did not consider liberalization in services. Third, it also did not consider the dynamic effects of trade liberalization: as I discuss in Chapter 4, the ways in which dynamic relations are integrated into CGEMs are neither microeconomically founded nor useful from an empirical point of view. Finally, these benefits may have been underestimated because the methodology used supposes that preferential schemes are fully implemented, and the trade elasticities used may be too low.

It is necessary to gauge the extent to which the expected benefits from trade liberalization can be underestimated. The review of the literature presented in Chapter 4 was done to confirm that the results obtained from my study are not outliers.

Modeling Trade Liberalization and Development Using CGEMs: A Survey

C GEM assessments of trade liberalization have multiplied. There are several explanations, including increased access to economic data, increased computational efficiencies, and development of the GTAP network. What is most surprising, however, is that the quantitative conclusions derived from CGEMs diverge.

Divergences among Assessments of Trade Liberalization Using CGEMs

Without being exhaustive, my survey covers 19 CGEM assessments of the impact of full trade liberalization on the world during the past 6 years[1] and 9 assessments of the impact of a potential Doha agreement. Appendix H provides synoptic tables on the assessments of full trade liberalization and of the DDA on world welfare and poverty.[2]

Convergent Conclusions

Before pointing out the divergences in these assessments and explaining their source, it is worthwhile to put an emphasis on a set of convergent conclusions of all these studies (some of these conclusions are highlighted in Table 4.1):

---

[1]The assessment carried out in Chapter 3 is included.

[2]In the case of World Bank (2004a; see Table H.1), it is a pro-poor scenario, which would imply the elimination of export subsidies, a decoupling of all domestic support, and a significant cut in tariffs: rich countries would be subject to a maximum tariff of 10 percent in agriculture (5 percent in industry), with an average target of 5 percent (1 percent). For developing countries, the caps would be 15 percent (10 percent), with an average of 10 percent (5 percent).

1. Full liberalization is beneficial. At the world level it increases welfare. This conclusion does not mean that all countries or all economic agents are better off. Liberalizing trade creates a "larger cake," but some can get smaller pieces than others; if efficient redistribution mechanisms are put in place, all agents could experience increased welfare.

2. Liberalizing agriculture is the main source of expected gains, accounting for about two-thirds of global gains. These gains come about because this sector contains a major part of current trade barriers. Furthermore, nearly all export subsidies and domestic support go to agriculture.[3]

3. Tariffs are by far the main source of distortions. They account for more than 90 percent of expected benefits in the case of full liberalization. This major political issue is confirmed by the assessment of the DDA. It prioritizes the elimination of export subsidies and a cut in domestic support, while pursuing modest objectives in terms of market access. For this reason, assessments of the DDA indicate only small welfare increases.

4. Developing countries could be large beneficiaries of these reforms. As their GDPs are lower, they would experience a higher rate of increase in their real incomes than would developed countries. In this sense, trade reform is progressive in that it increases real incomes of poor countries to a greater extent than those of other countries.

5. Liberalizing trade policies of developing countries is a major issue. It contributes about half of the expected benefits. This observation leads to another criticism of the DDA, because SDT could allow developing countries to liberalize less and LDCs to keep their trade policies unchanged.

These convergent conclusions are extremely important. Although the picture drawn by these models is not as favorable as the one that emerged a few years ago, it remains true that the global net expected effect is positive: trade liberalization has to be done even if parallel policies have to be implemented simultaneously. The other points in the above list detail the contents of positive world trade reform: it has to focus on agriculture and market access, and developing countries must reform their own economies as well.

Trade Pessimism?

Tables H.1 and H.2 reveal a major divergence in CGEM assessments. As far as full trade liberalization is concerned, the increase in world welfare ranges from 0.2 to 3.1 percent—a difference of a factor of 15! The impact on poverty headcount is

---

[3]Large gains in world welfare are expected from liberalization in services, but these estimates should be treated with great caution.

Table 4.1   Computable general equilibrium model assessments of full trade liberalization: Convergent conclusions (percent)

	Role of agriculture	Role of tariffs	Share of developing countries in benefits	Role of developing countries' policies
Dessus, Fukasaku, and Safadi (1999) scenario 1	n.a.	n.a.	22	n.a.
Dessus, Fukasaku, and Safadi (1999) scenario 2	n.a.	n.a.	43	45
Anderson et al. (2000)	65	n.a.	43	45
Diao, Somwaru, and Roe (2001) scenario 1	n.a.	n.a.	8	n.a.
Diao, Somwaru, and Roe (2001) scenario 2	n.a.	n.a.	38	n.a.
World Bank (2002) scenario 1	69	n.a.	52	55
World Bank (2002) scenario 2	71	n.a.	65	66
World Bank (2004a) scenario 1	66	n.a.	55	62
World Bank (2004a) scenario 2	69	n.a.	67	62
Cline (2004) scenario 1	57	n.a.	38	44
Cline (2004) scenario 2	n.a.	n.a.	47	n.a.
Beghin and Van der Mensbrugghe (2003)	69	99	56	n.a.
Anderson, Martin, and Van der Mensbrugghe, (2005a)	63	93	30	45
Francois, Van Meijl, and Van Tongeren (2005)	65	91	8	58
Hertel and Keeney (2005)	66	95	26	n.a.

Note: n.a., not available.

also divergent, as the number of people lifted from poverty ranges from 72 million to 440 million (a ratio of 1 to 6.1!) with an average of 219 million.[4] These numbers depict a rather contradictory picture of the effects of trade liberalization.[5]

Figure 4.1 ranks the estimations of world benefits from full trade liberalization in chronological order:[6] on average, the expected world welfare gain exhibits continuous decrease.[7] For example, from an average world welfare increase of 1.7 percent in 1999, the average estimate is 1.5 percent in 2002, 1.3 percent in 2004,

---

[4]In 2003, the number of people living in poverty (using the US$2.00 per day definition) was estimated at 2.8 billion (World Bank 2004b). Thus, the CGEM estimates suggest that full trade liberalization could decrease world poverty from 2.9 to 19.1 percent, with an average of 9.4 percent.

[5]In this survey, I do not include assessments of expected benefits from trade liberalization in services or from trade facilitation. These studies are rare, and although they shed light on a fundamental topic, the methodology needs further refinements. I included trade liberalization only in agriculture, as studied by Diao, Somwaru, and Roe (2001), but I did not use the results from Diao et al. (2005), because they account for the consequences for developing countries only.

[6]I excluded from this graphic the Diao, Somwaru, and Roe (2001) results, which focused only on agricultural liberalization.

[7]More precisely, the trend, calculated according to a linear regression, exhibits a decreasing slope.

Figure 4.1   Trade pessimism: Impact of full trade liberalization on world welfare

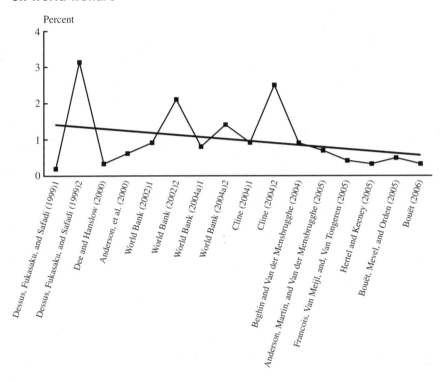

and 0.5 percent in 2005. Is the trade pessimism among trade economists getting ever stronger? If yes, is this conclusion justified?

Obviously, these results are not totally comparable. Real incomes can be defined in terms of either the 1997 dollar or the 2001 dollar. Furthermore, models can be static or dynamic. In the case of a dynamic model, the increase in supplies of productive factors are (endogenously or exogenously) taken into account, and in some simulations, even technical progress and related changes in factor productivity are included. Thus, the same rate of increase in real income, entailed by trade reform and applied to different bases, gives birth to different levels of assessments: comparing studies by rate of change in real income is more appropriate. It is even more reliable to compare results coming from the same model: Hertel and Keeney (2005) to Hertel (2000), for instance, or Anderson, Martin, and Van der Mensbrugghe (2005a) to the World Bank (2002, 2004a). This method of comparison results in a more accurate picture, but the main conclusion is the same: results are divergent, and the general trend is less trade optimism.

Figure 4.2   Trade pessimism: Impact of full trade liberalization on poverty headcount

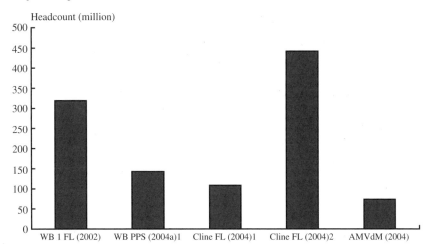

Notes: AMVdM, Anderson, Martin, and Van der Mensbrugghe; FL, full liberalization; PPS, pro-poor scenario; WB, World Bank. Numbers 1 and 2 indicate the scenario number for Cline and the World Bank calculations.

Figure 4.2 shows the impact of trade reform on poverty headcount. In 2004, Cline carried out two estimations, the second one being especially optimistic. Putting aside this second estimation, trade pessimism is rather confirmed. Finally, Table 4.2 indicates whether the assessments conclude that some regions or countries sustain welfare losses. Until 2000, most studies concluded that no nations suffered losses in terms of national real income from trade liberalization (a kind of *Mondialisation heureuse*[8]). Beginning with Dee and Hanslow (2000), more and more studies demonstrate welfare losses for countries. It is noteworthy that these are nearly all developing countries (with the exception of Canada, based on an assessment conducted in 2000).

The potential implications of the DDA have been also scrutinized, as laid out in Table H.2. A comparison of Tables H.1 and H.2 leads to the conclusion that the potential impact of the DDA is much smaller than the one resulting from full trade liberalization, which is one of the main conclusions of all these studies.

---

[8]A French expression for "fortunate globalization"; this qualification was made famous in France by an article by Alain Minc in the daily newspaper *Le Monde* in August 2001. It was a tentative description of globalization as a wonderful process giving benefits to everybody in all countries throughout the world.

Table 4.2   Trade pessimism: Potential losers from full trade liberalization

Reference	Potential loser
Dessus, Fukasaku, and Safadi (1999)	None
Dee and Hanslow (2000)	Canada, Mexico
Hertel (2000)	Other MENA countries
Diao, Somwaru, and Roe (2001) scenario 1	Mexico, Rest of the World
Diao, Somwaru, and Roe (2001) scenario 2	None
World Bank (2002) scenario 1	None
World Bank (2002) scenario 2	None
World Bank (2004a) scenario 1	None
World Bank (2004a) scenario 2	None
Cline (2004) scenario 1	Malaysia, Mexico
Cline (2004) scenario 2	China, Malaysia
Beghin and Van der Mensbrugghe (2003)	None
Anderson, Martin, and Van der Mensbrugghe (2005a)	None
Francois, Van Meijl, and Van Tongeren (2005)	China, India, South America
Hertel and Keeney (2005)	Bangladesh, Mozambique, Philippines, Rest of Latin America, Rest of Sub-Saharan Africa
Bouët, Mevel, and Orden (2005)	Argentina, Bangladesh, Canada, China, EU, Mexico, Mozambique, Southern African Customs Union, Venezuela, Zambia

Note: MENA, Middle East and North Africa.

Assessing the impact of the DDA using CGEMs also gives rise to divergences (Figure 4.3). The range of welfare variations for an agricultural Doha round is from 0.08 percent (Bouët et al. 2005) to 0.18 percent (Anderson, Martin, and Van der Mensbrugghe 2005a, scenario 1); it varies from 0.17 percent (Bouët, Mevel, and Orden 2005) to 0.51 percent (Fontagné, Guérin, and Jean 2005) for a complete round.

Why Do CGEM Assessments Diverge so Much?

Despite the similarities mentioned in the previous section, the divergences between these assessments and the increased pessimism about trade liberalization require further examination. It is easy to identify the potential sources of these divergences. Studies can differ by

1. the experiment conducted,
2. economic data used,
3. behavioral parameters assumed, and
4. theoretical features of the model.

The following sections examine each of these explanations in turn.

Figure 4.3   Trade uncertainty: Increase in world welfare for assessments of the Doha Development Agenda, 2005

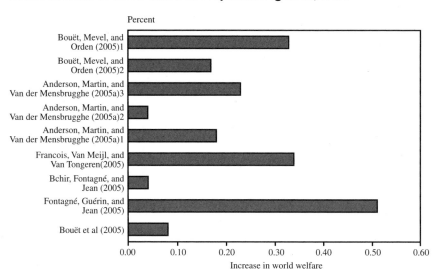

Percent

Increase in world welfare

Experiments Are Not the Same

The first explanation concerns the experiments. It does not only consider designed scenario but also the conduct of a pre-experiment and the offsetting of fiscal policies.

Full liberalization versus DDA.   Table H.1 considers only assessments of complete (in agriculture and industry) and full liberalization, with the exception of the study done by Diao, Somwaru, and Roe (2001), which assesses implications of liberalizing only agriculture. The experiments displayed in Table H.2 are tentative representations of a DDA only in industry, as examined by Bchir, Fontagné, and Jean (2005); in agriculture, as examined by Bouët et al. (2005); or in both sectors (Anderson, Martin, and Van der Mensbrugghe 2005a).

Obviously, DDA experiments might diverge, because at the time they were done, no study had complete and definitive information on the conclusion of this agenda. Most of these studies utilize the Harbinson proposal of May 2003 in agriculture (see Table 4.3); some use the Girard formula in industry. For more than 2 years after the start of the DDA, these formulas were the only quantitative proposals put forward by an official negotiator.

The Harbinson proposal is explained in Table 4.3. It defines several tiers with increased reduction rates when applied to initial tariffs.[9] For developed coun-

---

[9]Recall that these reduction rates are applied to bound duties.

tries,[10] for example, a tariff of 91 percent must be reduced by 60 percent, resulting in a tariff of 36.4 percent. The use of this formula is subject to criticism: in particular, it contains discontinuities. Some authors (such as Jean, Laborde, and Martin 2005) correct it, others (Bouët et al. 2005) apply it without any correction—which is the source of divergence in these assessments.

In trade negotiations, it often appears that the "devil is in the details." In other words, an ambitious package can be announced, but because it includes detailed and complicated clauses, its final impact on market access might be far from the one proclaimed. Three examples can illustrate this point:

1. Tariff rate quotas (TRQs) were implemented during the Uruguay Round to guarantee minimum access and safeguard the exports of some developing countries. There have been 1,371 TRQs implemented (for a complete presentation, see De Gorter and Sheldon 2000; Matthews and Laroche Dupraz 2001). A TRQ is composed of two tariffs (the inside quota tariff rate [IQTR] and the outside quota tariff rate [OQTR]) and a quota. Already difficult to ascertain the protective impact of a TRQ, it becomes even more hazardous to anticipate the way TRQs will be liberalized and the method by which countries will implement this reform. Trade negotiators could indeed decide to decrease TRQs, to expand quotas, or a combination of the two. At the national level, a government could modify the way quotas are administered,[11] which could have significant consequences on some developing countries.

2. The Geneva framework agreement, concluded on July 2004, includes a sensitive products clause: "Without undermining the overall objective of the tiered approach, members may designate an appropriate number, to be negotiated, of tariff lines to be treated as sensitive, taking account of existing commitments for these products" (see http://www.wto.org/english/tratop_e/dda_e /draft_ text_gc_dg_31july04_e.htm). This clause is so ambiguous that it is difficult to ascertain its consequences. Self-selection of tariff lines may imply that more protected products will be exempted from liberalization. Anderson, Martin, and Van der Mensbrugghe (2005a) demonstrated that even in the case of a low percentage of tariff lines admitted as sensitive products, these exceptions could considerably reduce the effects of liberalization. In Table H.2, the only difference between scenarios 1 and 2 carried out by Anderson, Martin, and Van der Mensbrugghe (2005a) is the inclusion of the sensitive and special products

---

[10]Recall that there is no formal WTO definition of developed or developing countries. Members announce for themselves whether they are developed or developing countries (see http://www.wto.org/ english/tratop_e/devel_e/d1who_e.htm).

[11]Quotas can be administered several ways: on a historical basis or on a first-come, first-served basis.

Table 4.3   The Harbinson proposal (percent)

Developed countries		Developing countries	
Initial tariff	Reduction rate	Initial tariff	Reduction rate
$t > 90$	60	$t > 120$	40
$15 < t \leq 90$	50	$60 < t \leq 120$	35
$t \leq 15$	40	$20 < t \leq 60$	30
		$t \leq 20$	25

clause on 2 percent of tariff lines. The associated world welfare gain is cut from US$75 billion to US$17 billion.

The importance of such a clause comes from the convex form of tariff distributions in OECD countries. Figure 4.4 illustrates this point, showing a distribution of bound tariffs in Switzerland, ranked in increasing order. In this country, as in the EU, Iceland, Japan, and Norway, protection is highly concentrated on a few products. Exempting a few lines of liberalization may have significant consequences. In 2001, the average Swiss bound duty in agriculture was 81.6 percent.[12] When applying the Harbinson proposal without the sensitive products clause, this average falls to 34.1 percent. If, on the contrary, a sensitive products clause is applied, exempting 2 percent of tariff lines from liberalization, and if in Switzerland, this room for maneuver is used on the highest duties in agriculture, the new bound duty average is 64.8 percent!

3. Specific tariffs, defined by monetary units per physical unit (U.S. dollars per ton or euros per kilogram), are numerous in rich countries' agricultural sectors. According to the MacMap-HS6 database, this trade barrier represents the totality of agricultural protection in Switzerland, and about three-quarters of it in the EU and Japan (see Bouët et al. 2008). If a proportional formula were applied, the existence of specific tariffs would not be a source of divergence. But it is all the more plausible that a progressive formula will be applied: larger cuts for higher initial tariffs, either by the Harbinson proposal or by a Swiss formula. It is, therefore, necessary to evaluate the ad valorem equivalent of a specific tariff. In the case of a tiered approach, this assessment is aimed at finding out which coefficient has to be applied. The transformation is also necessary in the case of a Swiss formula, as this approach only makes sense when applied to ad valorem duties.

---

[12]This average duty is here especially high, because ad valorem equivalents of specific tariffs, by far the most prominent instrument of protection in Switzerland, are calculated by dividing duties by world unit values, that is, relatively low unit values compared to national unit values of imports.

Figure 4.4   Bound duties for Switzerland, 2001

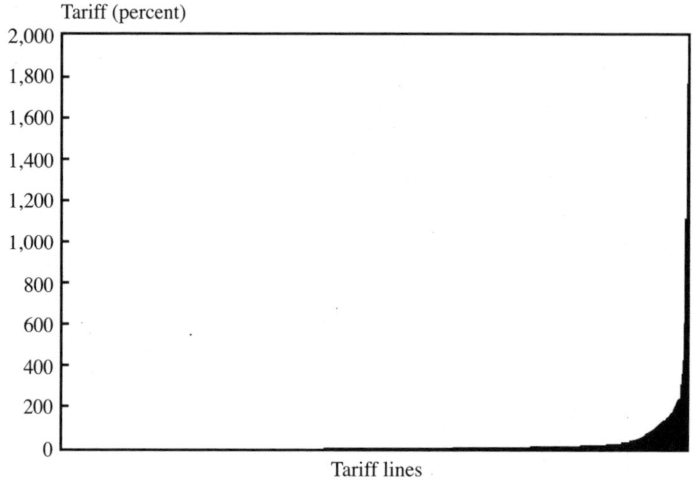

Tariff (percent)

Tariff lines

Calculating ad valorem equivalents of specific tariffs may seem straightforward, as it is only necessary to divide the specific duty by a unit value. However, the question remains: which unit value is to be used? For one product defined at the HS6 level, unit values of trade flows may greatly diverge, depending on whether they are taken at the national or the world level. The European Commission gives the example of fresh sausages, of which the unit value of European imports is €8/kg, while the world unit value is €2/kg (see Directorate General for Agricultural and Rural Development, European Commission 2005). The tariff applied by the EU is €1.5/kg; thus, the ad valorem equivalent is either 19 percent (using the European unit value) or 75 percent (using the world unit value). Because developed countries mostly import products of high quality, using a world unit value to calculate ad valorem equivalent systematically inflates the rate of liberalization. The construction of the MacMap-HS6 database clearly highlights this major issue (see Bouët et al. 2006, 2008). This difference in calculation was the main source of contention for trade negotiators during the first part of 2005.

From the above discussion, it clearly appears that a good assessment of the impact of the DDA must include consideration of not only the final agreement but the detailed way in which the agreement is implemented by each WTO member. Of course, it could be argued that in the case of full liberalization, this source of divergence disappears. Nevertheless, the need to define what full liberalization is and which distortions have to be eliminated remains. It may concern border measures (import duties and export subsidies) or domestic distortions; in the latter case, the definition is less obvious. One can choose measures to be eliminated on an institutional criterion, for example, those forbidden by the WTO. But it is also possible to include other programs that could have significant effects, contrary to what is expected from trade liberalization. For example the elimination of the European land set-aside program and the U.S. Conservation Reserve Program could contribute to a major expansion of land supply in these two countries and a substantial increase in their agricultural production.

There are other issues that may explain why experiments are not the same among different assessments of the effects of full trade liberalization. These are discussed in the next two subsections.

The issue of the pre-experiment definition.   Almost all studies use the GTAP database. The last available version (GTAP 6) is for 2001 and provides social accounting matrixes and trade flows for as many as 87 countries (or geographic zones) and 57 activities. Previous assessments used the GTAP 5, valid for 1997.

When studying trade liberalization, the reviewed studies usually suppose that it takes place in 2005 or 2006, implying an 8- or 9-year delay using the GTAP 5 version and a 4- or 5-year delay using GTAP 6. Whatever the effective date of liberalization, trade barriers have been reduced since both 1997 and 2001: the Uruguay Round has been definitively implemented with the phasing out of the Multi-Fibre Arrangement, some countries have entered the WTO and consequently reduced their tariff barriers (for example, China), some preferences have been granted to developing countries (for example, EBA and AGOA), and new regional agreements have been negotiated (such as between the United States and Morocco, between Chile and Mexico) or modified (enlargement of the EU to include 25 countries).

Applying a trade shock on a dataset that does not include all this information overstates the impact of full trade liberalization on trade flows, economic activity, and welfare. For this reason, most studies conduct a pre-experiment (for example, Beghin and Van der Mensbrugghe 2003; Anderson, Martin, and Van der Mensbrugghe 2005a; Bchir, Fontagné, and Jean 2005; Hertel and Keeney 2005). Several trade agreements, enforced during this transition, are simulated and applied to the initial database. Then the experiment involves simulating either full trade liberalization or the DDA on this modified database. Although concluding a full trade liberalization, implemented from 2005, would imply a world welfare gain of US$287 billion, Anderson, Martin, and Van der Mensbrugghe (2005a) demonstrate that the liberalization process that took place between 2001 and 2005 (the last implementation of the Uruguay Round, the end of the Multi-Fibre Arrangement, the access of China to the WTO, the enlargement of the EU by 10 countries from Eastern and Central Europe, the implementation of EBA and AGOA, and so on) has increased world welfare by US$54 billion—a gain of about 19 percent of the estimated gain of US$287 billion.

When modeling is done using recursive dynamics, a benchmark is determined: if the trade shock is applied over a period of 10 years, for example, the evolution of the world economy is simulated without any trade reform during this period, but with investments increasing the stock of capital and increases in labor supplies that are either exogenous (given a projected rate for that period) or endogenous (labor supply that is dependent on its real remuneration).[13] By using different benchmarks, however, the same trade reform will lead to different welfare gains. This sensitivity to the benchmark used is why comparing studies by rate of change (in percentages) is appropriate.

The issue of compensatory fiscal policies.   Alongside the elimination of trade distortions, fiscal policies are frequently implemented in these assessments that could lead to divergent conclusions. Two reasons may be invoked for including fiscal reforms simultaneously with trade reforms in liberalization assessments:

1. The fiscal issue is a major concern in developing countries, where corruption and tax evasion are prominent. As income and sales taxes do not yield sufficient public receipts, taxing imports has become a key source of revenue for the public sector. Table I.1 in Appendix I indicates the importance of import taxes as a proportion of GDP in the 85 countries and/or zones of the GTAP 6 database. In developing countries, these taxes represent from 0.4 percent of the domestic GDP in Botswana up to 4.3 percent in Tunisia. When implementing full trade liberalization, it may be unrealistic to neglect any offsetting fiscal instruments (which can be more or less distorting). Even the implementation of the DDA could reduce fiscal receipts.

2. For more than 60 years (the Stolper-Samuelson theorem was been published in 1941), liberalizing trade was been considered to affect the income distribution inside a country. Thus, it can be argued that reducing trade barriers increases economic efficiency (it increases the size of the pie) but it also modifies the way in which income is distributed (the way the pie is split). As a matter of fact, it could be argued that the effects of free trade have to be corrected by fiscal policy. This issue is all the more important now, because the stated objective of the current round of negotiation is poverty alleviation. Poverty results from low factor remuneration and/or high consumer prices. If prices of commodities, the production of which requires an intensive utilization of unskilled labor,

---

[13]Land supply can also be modified as its real remuneration changes.

are increased, the activity in this sector is enhanced and the demand for and remuneration of this factor is elevated; this last result contributes to poverty alleviation. On the other hand, augmented consumer prices have adverse effects on the poor people who buy these commodities. One way of tackling this issue is to use fiscal instruments.

The idea that trade liberalization should be accompanied by a fiscal policy is consistent. But it represents yet another source of divergence among the assessments of expected benefits.

Data Are Not the Same

The utilization of different data leads logically to different assessments. Nearly all assessments use the GTAP database on consumption, production, and international trade. But divergences may stem from the use of different databases on market access and domestic support, even though today modelers are increasingly using the same information.

Data on market access.   Data on market access have greatly evolved within a few years. It might be one of the major sources of reduced optimism about the expected benefits from trade liberalization. Three improvements are significant:

1. The main databases take into account trade preferences and regional agreements.
2. Ad valorem equivalents of specific tariffs and tariff rate quotas are calculated.
3. Simulation of multilateral trade negotiation accounts for the interaction of bound and applied duties.

MacMap-HS6 is a four-dimensional database on market access (importing country, products, exporting country, and instrument of protection). It includes all preferential schemes and regional agreements between different countries.[14] The base period for MacMap-HS6 is 2001, and the commodity coverage includes 5,111 products (Harmonized System at the 6-digit level, or HS6). It includes ad valorem duties, specific duties, compound duties, TRQs, and antidumping duties, and calculates ad valorem equivalents of all these protective instruments. It measures market access to 163 countries by 208 partners.

The objective of global trade negotiations is the reduction of bound duties. Thus, an accurate assessment of the impact of a multilateral trade reform must take into account the interplay among bound, most-favored-nation (MFN) applied,

---

[14]For a complete description of the MacMap-HS6 database, see Bouët et al. (2006, 2008).

and preferential duties. To complement MacMap-HS6, the CEPII has recently constructed a dataset on bound duties for 2001. The data on market access from MacMap-HS6 have been included in the GTAP database.[15]

The MacMap-HS6 database is now the main reference for measuring market access in general equilibrium analyses; it has resulted in a downward assessment of the level of protection throughout the world, because it includes all preferential schemes and regional agreements, instead of basing border protection uniquely on MFN tariffs. Obviously, this methodology implies that trade preferences are fully utilized, whereas such preferential schemes (and to a lesser extent, free trade agreements) have been frequently criticized because of their lack of efficiency. These agreements always include rules of origin to avoid trade deflection. The stringency of these rules has been pointed out. Initial empirical assessments were very pessimistic about the rate of utilization of these schemes (Brenton 2003; Brenton and Manchin 2003; Brenton and Ikezuki 2004), but new methodologies and studies have recently demonstrated that these preferences are rather well utilized by exporters from developing countries, especially in agriculture (Wainio and Gibson 2003; Candau, Fontagné, and Jean 2004; Candau and Jean 2005).

Assessing the impact of trade liberalization requires taking into account the interplay between MFN duties and preferential duties and, as far as the DDA is concerned, the interactions between these duties and bound tariffs. This consideration results in a reduced estimation of the expected benefits of liberalization. Jean, Laborde, and Martin (2005) calculate that taking into account applied tariffs instead of MFN tariffs in agriculture decreases border protection by 30 percent (calculated as (24–17)/24; see Figure 4.5), whereas the binding overhang is greater than 13 percent. Preferences (difference between MFN-applied and applied tariffs) are large in developed countries, whereas they are very small in LDCs. In fact, the gap between bound and MFN duties is large in the latter and small in the former (it is even larger in LDCs than in middle-income countries).

Data on domestic support.   Data on domestic support can also greatly differ across studies. Domestic support is a distortion, the definition and economic impact of which varies much more than that of tariffs: it can act on production, on intermedi-

---

[15]The GTAP data on protection are based on MacMap data at the HS6 level, but the way data are aggregated up to the GTAP disaggregation level is different from the MacMap methodology. GTAP uses a system of weights based on national imports, whereas the MacMap weighting system is based on imports from a reference group. As a result, GTAP understates the actual level of protection but includes consistent data with respect to tariff receipts. This difference is of course another source of divergence between assessments using the GTAP method of tariff aggregation (Anderson, Martin, and Van der Mensbrugghe 2005a,b; Hertel and Keeney 2005) and evaluations using the MacMap method (Bouët et al. 2005).

Figure 4.5   Bound and applied agricultural tariff rates, by region, 2001

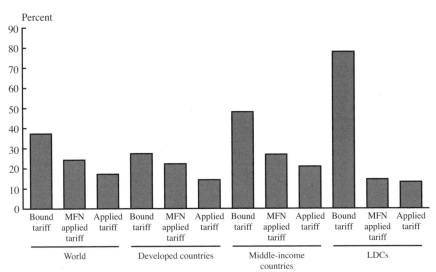

Source: Jean, Laborde, and Martin (2005).
Note: LDCs, least-developed countries.

ate inputs, on farmers' income, on capital or land, and so forth; it can have a direct or indirect effect on production (coupled or decoupled); it can be bound or not.

Bouët et al. (2005) distinguish among market price support, output subsidies, capital subsidies, variable input subsidies, land subsidies, and decoupled subsidies in OECD countries and China. Even if decoupled subsidies are modeled to have an indirect effect on production, taking into account this form of domestic support reduces the impact of liberalization on world prices. Some programs even have a negative impact on production (such as the land set-aside program in Europe, Conservation Reserve Program in the United States), so that their elimination would entail an increase in domestic production.

Recent research has also pointed to a "binding overhang" phenomenon in domestic support programs as developed countries' governments have consolidated these measures and effective subsidies are deemed inferior. Anderson, Martin, and Van der Mensbrugghe (2005a,b) demonstrated that very large reductions in bound support are needed before any reduction in actual support would take place.

Different decompositions by sector and trading zone.   CGEMs are sophisticated representations of the world economy. Modeling consumption, production, and trade of several products in several trading zones requires solving a very large system of equations. Thus, it is necessary to identify a limited number of sectors and trading zones, because the number of equations increases exponentially when these parameters are increased: some equations have up to four dimensions.

But reducing the number of sectors and trading zones is costly: if the size of the distortion differs among sectors or trading zones, it decreases the cost of protection, because this cost is proportional to the square of the tariff. Thus, two studies assessing the impact of the same trade reform with the same model and the same data, but with different product and geographic decompositions will produce different welfare results. The choice of geographic and sector decompositions depends largely on the questions being analyzed.

Behavioral Parameters Are Not the Same

Welfare effects created by liberalization depend crucially on the elasticity of substitution between domestic and imported goods and on elasticities of substitution among imports from different sources. Let us consider first the case of unilateral liberalization. This case is modeled in a partial equilibrium analysis in Figure 4.6. In the left panel, domestic supply and demand are represented. Initially, the world price is π_1, and the study country imposes an ad valorem import duty t_1. The domestic price is therefore $\pi_1(1 + t_1)$, leading to a domestic supply O_1 and a domestic demand D_1. This gap $(D_1 - O_1)$ creates imports, represented in the right panel, where the initial equilibrium is at A, the intersection of import demand for a t_1 tariff $M(t_1)$ and export supply X.

Cutting import tariff implies an upward shift in import demand $M(t_2)$. The new equilibrium is at B. The net effect is the difference between the gray areas (allocative efficiency gains) and the black area in the graph (terms-of-trade loss—in this case, it is a terms-of-trade loss because import prices are raised). In Figure 4.6, because of a highly elastic export supply, the world price increases little. This result is very beneficial for the importing country, because the negative impact of liberalization for this country is small. Initial imports are paid by the country at a higher price: this loss is equal to the black area $(\pi_2 - \pi_1)(D_1 - O_1)$.

Consider the case of a decrease in trade elasticity. In Figure 4.6, if the slope of X is made more vertical, domestic liberalization implies a smaller increase in imports and a higher increase in world price. Gains in domestic welfare are smaller. So in the case of unilateral liberalization, the effects on welfare are twofold. First, they are caused by an increase in domestic imports, which reflects the replacement of domestic production by more competitive foreign supply, and domestic consumption profits from lower consumption prices. Simultaneously, tariff revenue is modified by an increase in imports (positive effect) and a decrease of the taxation rate (negative). Second, they are a result of the change in the world price; when a commodity is imported, a cut in tariff increases the world price, leading to negative

Figure 4.6   A partial equilibrium representation of unilateral liberalization

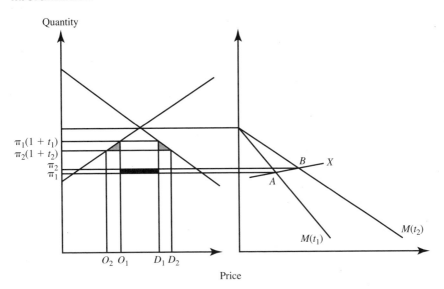

welfare effects. For the same change in imports, a high trade elasticity implies a smaller augmentation of world price, and thus, larger welfare effects.

In the case of multilateral liberalization, terms-of-trade effects can be obtained on exports as access to foreign markets is modified. Exporters clearly receive a higher price for their exports from the liberalization of foreign economies. This result is of course a positive evolution of terms of trade. But liberalization can decrease export prices: for example, if initially preferences have been granted for a market in specific countries, erosion of these preferences implies lower export prices for these erstwhile preferred exporters, stemming from increased competition.

Finally, at the world level, terms-of-trade effects eliminate one another, and welfare effects only come from the elimination of domestic distortions (in a framework of perfect competition). Eliminating distortions has large welfare effects when import demands are highly elastic.

In conclusion, trade elasticities are key parameters in global trade modeling. Unfortunately, there is no consensus on their value; moreover, they vary with the level of product disaggregation. On average, the GTAP network provides relatively low trade elasticities, even if recent developments have provided higher estimations of these parameters (see Hertel et al. 2003). In contrast, Harrison, Rutherford, and Tarr (henceforth the HRT model; see, for example, Harrison, Rutherford, and Tarr 1997, 2001) use much higher trade elasticities than the GTAP (see, for example,

Harrison, Rutherford, and Tarr 2001). LINKAGE elasticities are intermediate: on average they are 35 percent higher than the GTAP values but are 75 percent higher in agriculture. This point is a direct and important explanation of the divergences highlighted in Appendixes A and B. Cline's (2004) study uses the HRT model and obtains, therefore, higher welfare effects from full trade liberalization. Anderson, Martin and Van der Mensbrugghe (2005a,b) obtain intermediate results; using GTAP elasticities, they even demonstrate that the utilization of various trade elasticities is the main explanation for differences in assessing welfare effects.

Theoretical Assumptions Are Not the Same

The final source of divergence concerns theoretical features of the model. It is nearly impossible to be exhaustive on this topic, because modelers have to make numerous theoretical choices. This section focuses on the main theoretical assumptions used in assessing the impact of trade liberalization.

Perfect versus imperfect competition.   CGEM can adopt either a perfect or imperfect competition framework, or a combination of these two features in different productive sectors. In the latter case, industry and services are very often characterized by imperfect competition, whereas in agriculture it is assumed to be perfect.

Imperfect competition implies new sources of welfare gains from trade liberalization. Selling on a larger market, economies of scale are better utilized. Prices decrease. Furthermore, there is greater product variety in a larger market, meaning that consumers are better off. Nevertheless, imperfect competition is more difficult to model. First, when using the traditional CES function, the price elasticity of demand is not constant, and specifications of markup are complex. Second, imperfect competition with horizontal product differentiation requires a lot of information, particularly on product substitutability, scale economies, and competition intensity. Because these parameters are linked by the zero-profit condition in each sector, only two of these parameters are required from an external source, the third one being calibrated. It nevertheless demands detailed information about the economic structure in a multicountry multiproduct model. The intensive demand for information explains why this feature is not systematically adopted in all CGEMs, even though it is clearly more realistic.

Modeling the factor market.   A key feature of CGEMs is the assumptions attached to the productive factor markets. In a model designed to describe short-term consequences of trade liberalization, factors are often supposed to be immobile across sectors. When, conversely, the long-term consequences of openness are assessed, perfect mobility is often assumed. Between these two extremes, numerous assumptions are feasible: some primary factors (for example, land, natural resources) are naturally less mobile than others, but even in this respect, assumptions can differ across studies, because one can suppose either complete sector immobility of land or mobility across agricultural activities.

A key issue is labor mobility: it can be supposed that labor is either perfectly mobile (only one price of labor in the entire economy); perfectly immobile (as many wages as the number of sectors in the economy); or that there is an imperfect mobility of labor between agricultural and nonagricultural activities,[16] but that mobility is perfect within each activity.

Trade liberalization implies a change in the relative prices of goods in an economy. Thus, it must entail a reallocation of productive factors from those sectors whose relative prices are declining to sectors whose prices are increasing. In doing so, the economy is becoming specialized in activities where it has a comparative advantage—it increases its real income. This reallocation is all the more efficient if factors are mobile. So studies with different assumptions on productive factor markets yield different results on welfare and real income augmentations.

Static versus dynamic modeling.   A central feature that distinguishes the various CGEMs is whether they are static or dynamic. When accounting for dynamics, trade liberalization might affect income, saving and investment, and capital (or other primary factors, such as skilled labor or land) accumulation rate. The rate at which these factors grow can be exogenously determined, or this mechanism can be endogenously defined: the split of active population between skilled and unskilled can be determined, for example, by the ratio of real remunerations or can be fixed by simple extrapolation. Technical progress can be accounted for; factor productivity can increase exogenously or total factor productivity can depend on specific variables (trade openness) and the like. Finally, either the dynamics can be recursive (the model is solved for consecutive periods, the resultant value of each variable from one period is included as the initial value of the next period, and there are no expectations) or it can be fully dynamic with intertemporal specifications (economic agents anticipate incomes and prices of subsequent periods, and these expectations influence the way in which markets are equilibrated in the current period).

In a dynamic CGEM, a baseline is simulated: the model is solved without any trade reform for the chosen number of periods, with accumulation of production factors. Then the trade reform is simulated: trade reform is assessed by comparison between the baseline and the simulation. Dynamic modeling can greatly affect the way trade liberalization is assessed. First, the dynamic mechanism increases the size of the world economy, such that one must compare the rates of changes in welfare

---

[16]To represent this imperfect immobility, a CET is often assumed between these different types of activities. Thus, labor is allocated among the different activities according to the ratio of remunerations.

(and not monetary amounts) among several studies. Second, trade reform may have a direct effect on the accumulation of productive factors. Traditionally, investment is determined by savings. The savings rate can be fixed, in which case investment increases when real income increases. This result is a positive effect of trade reform on capital accumulation and welfare. The savings rate can otherwise be determined by the real remuneration of capital. In this case, trade reform has a magnified impact on economies in which this remuneration is augmented either by a specialization effect in capital-intensive sectors or by an increased profitability stemming from better exploitation of scale economies. Otherwise, trade liberalization can affect the real remuneration of land (and thus the land supply; for example, in LINKAGE and MIRAGE) and the ratio of skilled to unskilled wages (and thus the split of active population between skilled and unskilled labor).

A key assumption explaining divergence among studies (displayed in Tables H.1 and H.2) certainly comes from the relation between total factor productivity and trade openness. Recalling the specification adopted in the World Bank's *Global Economic Prospects* (World Bank 2002, 2004a) and in Dessus, Fukasaku, and Safadi (1999), let γ_i^e be the growth in the sector's productivity stemming from the change in openness, E_i be the exports of sector i, and X_i output. The relation is assumed to take the form:

$$\gamma_i^e = \chi_i^0 \left(\frac{E_i}{X_i} \right)^{\eta_i}, \tag{26}$$

where χ_i^0 is calibrated using a specific rule[17] and η_i is the elasticity. This relation mechanically amplifies the expected benefits of trade liberalization.

Several mechanisms are supposed to operate positively on factor productivity when an economy is progressively exposed to international competition. As firms export more, they are supposed to learn new technologies through comparison with foreign competitors and to improve their production process to match international standards. Moreover, firms can react to more competition by increasing their efforts in research and development (R&D), which affects positively the productivity of all factors.

Are these assumptions pertinent, and is it reasonable to include them in global trade modeling? In fact, these mechanisms are realistic. Enhanced competition increases X efficiency and might be a direct incentive to do more R&D. Comparison of different production processes is a good way to improve efficiency. So trade open-

---

[17] For example, in the World Bank's *Global Economic Prospects* (2002, 2004a), it is supposed that trade openness explains 40 percent of total factor productivity growth.

ness should increase factor productivity. But the way in which this relation has been introduced in CGEMs may be subject to criticism for several reasons.

First, equation (26) has no microeconomic foundations, as opposed to all other elements in a CGEM.[18] Microeconomic models of international trade under oligopolistic competition can imply adverse effects; for example, Reitzes (1991) and Bouët (2001) demonstrate that protectionism can increase domestic R&D, depending on the instrument utilized (tariff versus quota).

Second, it can be considered as an ad hoc element introduced in a CGEM that studies the impact of trade liberalization. Obviously, introducing a function that is not microeconomically founded in such an evaluation leads to increasing factor productivity with trade openness and automatically amplifies the efficiency effect of trade openness.

Third, this relation is ad hoc; it does not allow any conclusion on which countries, sectors, or productive factors could be the first beneficiaries of trade liberalization or of a potentially positive impact on productivity. After all, if greater openness increases factor productivity, it makes sense that this relation is not the same for all countries, all sectors, and all factors. For example, the extent to which openness increases a country's productivity may depend on the domestic endowment in human capital.

A CGEM studying the impact of trade liberalization delivers plenty of information: the impacts of domestic reform on domestic efficiency, of modified import prices, of changes in market access on export prices, of changes in real remunerations of factor prices on their accumulation, of trade liberalization on economies of scale and differentiation of products, and so forth. These mechanisms (and their interplay) represent the most interesting relations in a CGEM. On these topics, equation (26) does not supply information, because it does not include any contrasting effect or differentiated impact of trade openness on factor productivity. Furthermore, it can be sufficiently strong to offset all negative mechanisms previously cited.

Another way of modeling dynamic effects is the steady state version of the HRT model (see Cline 2004). The idea is to increase the stock of capital until the rate of return is back to its preliberalization level. This method can be justified by the following idea. In the long term, firms are supposed to benefit from the new opportunities created by a much larger market, so that they invest until the rate of return comes back to a normal level. This idea makes sense, but, obviously, augmented capital creates more activity and increases the real remuneration of all

---

[18]There are also specifications between trade and productivity with microeconomic consideration in the literature. For example, in the Carnegie model (see Polaski 2006), there is a specification that links imported technology transfer (via imports of capital goods and intermediate inputs from rich countries to poor ones) and total factor productivity.

other factors. It automatically amplifies expected benefits from liberalization, and the microeconomic behavior of firms is not explicitly modeled.

Adopting specific theoretical assumptions can lead to very specific results. The Carnegie model (Polaski 2006) supposes that in developing countries' industrial sectors, real unskilled labor's remuneration is fixed (because of unemployment), whereas agricultural wages are perfectly flexible and ensure full employment. A migration function describes the rural–urban reallocation of this productive factor, and its intensity depends on the difference between agricultural and urban wages.

When a developing country participates in a liberalization agreement, industry can be negatively shocked by the increased openness. Less demand for domestic industrial products leads to less demand for labor in this sector. This reduction in turn implies migration and, in agriculture, an increase in the labor supply means, other things being equal, a reduction in the equilibrium wage. Thus in this developing country, trade liberalization leads to less employment in the industrial sector and reduced wages in agriculture. But if the industrial sector expands because of augmented exports, employment is increased and a migration from rural areas to urban areas occurs, decreasing labor supply in agriculture and so pushing up agricultural wages. Trade liberalization results in more industrial employment and increased agricultural wages in this country.

These scenarios result in highly contrasting fortunes for developing countries, depending on the impact of trade reform on demand for domestic industrial products. Furthermore, there is no equilibrating force, because the model is calibrated to perpetuate fixed real wages in industry. In contrast, in a flexible wage model, competitiveness in the industrial sector is progressively eroded as industrial wages are increased.

Evaluating the Impact of Trade Liberalization on Poverty

Evaluating the potential impact of trade liberalization on poverty has been done according to various methodologies. The first method is the one referenced in World Bank (2002, 2004a) and in Cline (2004). It allows for worldwide assessments of the impact on poverty. It estimates (or uses) a parameter known as poverty elasticity: this parameter is supposed to express how poverty incidence is reduced when an index representative of what poor people gain is augmented.

For example, the World Bank (2002, 2004a) assessments utilize results from a CGEM to calculate an index representative of poor people's real incomes; it is the remuneration of unskilled labor deflated by a consumption price index composed of food products and clothing. At the world level, the same elasticity is applied to calculate the impact on poverty headcounts. World Bank (2002) concluded that full trade liberalization would imply an increase of $x = 8.4$ percent in the real wages of unskilled labor in Sub-Saharan Africa. Because the poverty elasticity is −2, the report concluded that the poverty headcount in this region would decrease by 16.8 percent (that is, 2x) if full trade liberalization were to be applied.

This framework can only approximate the relation between trade liberalization and poverty for two reasons. First, the incomes of poor people are affected not only by remuneration of unskilled labor, but also by remuneration of skilled labor, capital, land, natural resources, and transfers. Applying the same elasticity at the world level is questionable. The relation between trade reform and poverty depends on the distribution of income among the population, the source of income at different levels of income, the reaction of economic agents to trade shocks, and so forth. Each of these relations is country specific. This criticism has been taken into account by the World Bank, which is now using country-specific poverty elasticity to assess the impact of liberalization. It partly explains why the recent assessment by Anderson, Martin, and Van der Mensbrugghe (2005c) is less optimistic in terms of poverty alleviation (see Figure 4.2).

The second reason is that because variation in the real wages of unskilled labor is calculated for every trading region of the CGEM, these regions have to be defined carefully so that they are homogenous as far as this relation is concerned. Furthermore, applying the concept of poverty elasticity gives the impression that the relation between trade openness and poverty alleviation is mechanical. According to this scheme, once liberalization is implemented, an increase in the real remuneration of unskilled labor occurs, and poverty is reduced to an extent that depends only on the strength of the shock.

Evidently, this scenario is not the case. Trade openness has contrasting distributive effects. Traditionally, it increases real remuneration of unskilled labor in developing countries, as their endowment of this factor is abundant. But other components of poor people's incomes can be negatively affected, particularly transfers stemming from shrinking tariff receipts. Furthermore, factors are not, especially in the short term, perfectly mobile across sectors. For example, unskilled labor can be imperfectly (or not at all) mobile between agricultural and nonagricultural activities. This variability in mobility gives rise to differences in remuneration of unskilled labor in a developing country. In this case, trade liberalization may have adverse effects on unskilled labor, depending on the sector where it is utilized. For example, Cororaton and Cockburn (2004) demonstrate that opening the Philippines to world competition can be beneficial to urban poor households and harmful for rural poor households.

Finally, stating that x million people are lifted out of poverty could be understood as both a quantitative and qualitative statement. Quantitatively, it means that x percent fewer persons have an income of less than US$2.00 per day. Qualitatively, the end of poverty might mean a profound change in the way of life. Even if the construction of statistical indicators requires the definition of arbitrary thresholds, the reader should keep in mind that this qualitative aspect might be neglected for people whose income just passes over this threshold.

Cline (2004) utilizes a marginally improved methodology aimed at evaluating country-specific poverty elasticities. He supposes that:

1. In all developing countries the income distribution is lognormal.
2. Full trade liberalization implies economic growth that is neutral from the point of view of the income distribution: it changes the average income but has no effect on income dispersion.
3. Poor people's incomes are composed of 90 percent remuneration of unskilled labor and 10 percent transfers.
4. The evolution of transfers is strictly parallel to the evolution of domestic welfare.
5. Poor people have the same consumption basket as the general population.

The first two hypotheses imply that the share of poor people in a population can be expressed as a function of the ratio of poor people's income to the average income and of the dispersion parameter (which is constant). The last three assumptions provide an expression of this ratio.

Note that economic growth changes income inequality,[19] and poor people's incomes are also affected by change in the remuneration of capital, land, natural resources, and skilled labor. Furthermore, there is no systematic reason to think that evolution of transfers is parallel to the evolution of national welfare, and consumption baskets depend on income levels: thus, assumptions 4 and 5 are not justified. Finally, as for the World Bank (2002, 2004a), Cline's (2004) method also posits a mechanical relation between trade openness and poverty.

The steady state model used by Cline (2004) automatically amplifies the impact of trade liberalization on poverty. As capital is raised, real remuneration of all other productive factors is augmented (in particular, unskilled labor's wages). Given that unskilled labor's wages represent 90 percent of poor people's incomes, the effect on poverty in this case is greatly reinforced.

There are other ways in which CGEMs can be utilized to study the relationship between trade liberalization and poverty. Traditionally, to obtain information on final consumption, CGEMs depict the behavior of a single household. Household disaggregation allows the study of how income distribution is affected by (trade) reform. The simplest way to do this is to model the behavior of several households

---

[19]A famous empirical demonstration of this point is the Kuznets (1955) curve.

using an exogenous variable: Kahn (1997) prioritizes a rural versus urban distinction, whereas Hertel et al. (2000) emphasize the main sources of income (unskilled labor, skilled labor, and capital). Traditionally, the number of households is limited, from 10 (Levin 2000) to 24 (Devarajan and Van der Mensbrugghe 2000), and a distribution of income for each representative household is postulated. The mean and total incomes of a household group are explained by the model, and dispersion is assumed to be constant. The adopted distribution functions are usually the lognormal or the Paretian distributions, even if they are of little empirical value.

Recent developments have prioritized two dimensions:

1. Thousands of households may be introduced in a CGEM (Cogneau and Robilliard 2000; Cockburn 2001; Cororaton and Cockburn 2004). This practice allows all information from household surveys to be retained and avoids the necessity of a theoretical simplification (treating within-group income dispersion as constant). But CGEM microsimulation is often done at the expense of other simplifications, such as a reduced number of sectors.

2. Hertel et al. (2000) utilize results coming from a multicountry CGEM on commodity and factor prices to feed a postsimulation framework that uses information on prices and income and simulates the demand response to these changes. These simulation techniques are very useful, because they account for a multisector, multifactor framework where agents' reactions to reform are simulated and the general equilibrium effect is taken into account. Furthermore, a policy study can be designed to describe the conditions under which losers can be compensated (see, for example, Harrison, Rutherford, and Tarr 2001).

These studies show that trade liberalization might have a positive effect on national welfare while having contrasting effects on domestic agents. Trade liberalization might alleviate poverty, but in several cases it increases it. Hertel et al. (2000), for example, show that if multilateral trade liberalization decreases poverty in several developing countries, it has the opposite effect in Brazil, Chile, and Thailand. Unfortunately, they cannot provide a worldwide estimation of the impact of full trade liberalization on poverty, unless results are extrapolated across developing countries. Thus, assessing the impact of trade liberalization on poverty is a very difficult task, which needs to account for the impact on commodity prices and factor incomes at a very detailed level.

For the effect of trade liberalization on real income, four explanations of divergences on how trade liberalization increases world real income have been presented. Pre-experiments are now systematically integrated into studies, and measurement of market access always accounts for preferential schemes and regional agreements. Two methodological choices—sources of major divergence—remain: the level of

Armington elasticities and the integration of a dynamic relationship between trade openness and total factor productivity. There may be other sources of divergence (such as data on market access or the conducting of a pre-experiment), but these sources have a smaller impact. To test these explanations of diverging results, a sensitivity analysis is carried out using the CGEM framework of Chapter 3.

A Sensitivity Analysis

Here I test the plausibility of the four rationales presented in this study to explain why literature on the impact of trade liberalization produces divergent conclusions. These rationales have already been discussed in detail earlier in this chapter: (1) experiments are not the same; (2) data are not the same; (3) behavioral parameters are not the same; and (4) theoretical features are not the same. To test these rationales, this section describes new simulations of full trade liberalization, each with one modification (see also Anderson, Martin, and Van der Mensbrugghe 2005a).

Figure 4.7 shows the main conclusion of this section. The central experiment, as described in the previous section, concluded that full trade liberalization would entail a 0.33 percent increase in world real income. The four modeling options shown in Figure 4.7 produced the following results. (1) Neglecting the pre-experiment (that is, not accounting for the trade liberalization that occurred from 2001 to 2005 before testing the impact of full trade liberalization) raises this rate of change by 36 percent (up to 0.45 percent). (2) Basing the simulations on a database with no preferential schemes, results in a 24 percent higher increase in world welfare (up to 0.41 percent). (3) Using the LINKAGE trade elasticities augments world real income by 33 percent (up to 0.44 percent). (4) Finally, including a positive relation between trade openness and total factor productivity raises the rate of change in the world welfare by 79 percent (up to 0.59 percent). Later in this chapter I check whether other theoretical features (such as exogenous or endogenous land supply, imperfect or perfect competition) or empirical choices (such as a different database for distortions, different product and sector disaggregations) also have an impact. Appendixes J–M contain detailed information about the results obtained from these alternative simulations.

Different Experiments: No Pre-Experiment

If a pre-experiment had not been implemented in the central experiment, the results would show a 0.45 percent augmentation in world real income implied by full trade liberalization (see Appendix J). Figure 4.8 highlights the welfare gains or losses by zones. The broad picture is unchanged; nevertheless, taking into account the end of the Uruguay Round raises allocation efficiency gains in numerous countries (such as Argentina, Canada, and India). The main difference comes from China's accession

Figure 4.7   The rate of change in world welfare compared to the central experiment

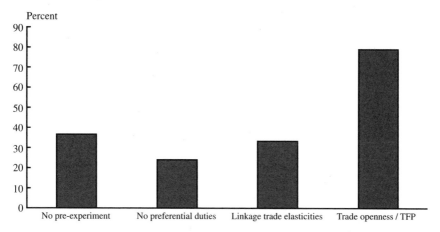

Percent

Figure 4.8   Welfare gains by region: Full trade liberalization from 2001

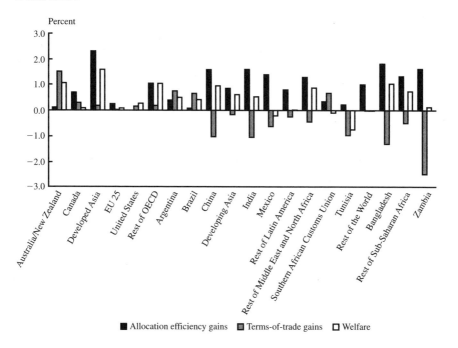

Percent

■ Allocation efficiency gains   ▦ Terms-of-trade gains   ☐ Welfare

to the WTO, which implies a significant cut in Chinese protection and large allocation efficiency gains (1.6 percent instead of 0.8 percent). Furthermore, the end of
the Multi-Fibre Arrangement opens access to American, Canadian, and European
markets. It entails a reduction in export prices for countries that were beneficiaries
of preferential access in the textiles and wearing apparel sectors.

As the reductions in tariff protection become larger, world agricultural prices
increase. This trend accentuates contrasts in terms of trade, with larger gains for
some (Argentina, Australia/New Zealand, and Brazil) and larger losses for others
(India and Zambia).

Different Data: MFN versus Preferential Duties

The second sensitivity analysis measures the extent to which the complete inclusion of preferential schemes modifies expected benefits. To study this aspect, tariffs
are changed in the initial database so that nonreciprocal preferences granted by
Canada, Developed Asia, the EU, Rest of OECD, and the United States to developing countries are removed. In other words, only regional agreements and MFN
tariffs are kept.

As expected, the positive impact on world welfare is bolstered: from 0.33 percent with preferential duties to 0.41 percent without (see Appendix K). Developing
countries are the main beneficiaries (Figure 4.9). This gain is large in the case of
Tunisia (which has preferential access to the European market in industry) and
Sub-Saharan Africa (including SACU and Zambia).

Why? As previously explained, eroded preferences mean deterioration in terms
of trade. In the absence of preferences, these countries profit from terms-of-trade
gains or reduced deterioration (see the cases of Bangladesh, Brazil, Mexico, Rest of
Sub-Saharan Africa, SACU, and Zambia by comparing Table 3.5 and Table K.2
in Appendix K).

In the case of Tunisia, allocation efficiency gains and welfare increase are much
larger. When the Euro–Mediterranean partnership is not taken into account, full
liberalization entails a significant increase in textiles and wearing apparel exports to
Europe. Reallocation of productive factors is needed to carry out this augmented
industrial production, while domestic prices have to increase to keep the current
account constant. Domestic agricultural liberalization completes this picture, and
increases in domestic agrifood imports are much larger than in the case of the main
experiment. Thus, there are greater gains in allocation efficiency for the same degree
of tariff elimination.[20]

---

[20]Allocation efficiency gains are proportional to the square of the tariff and the variation in imports.

Figure 4.9   Welfare gains by region: Full trade liberalization without nonreciprocal preferential schemes

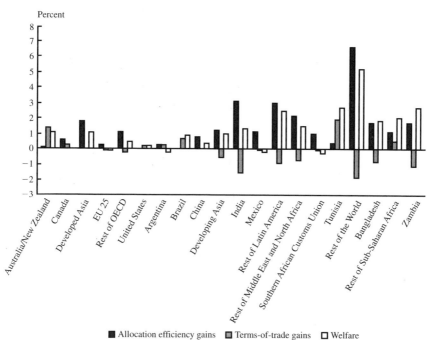

■ Allocation efficiency gains   ▣ Terms-of-trade gains   □ Welfare

The only developing countries that now lose from full trade liberalization are Argentina (because of overspecialization in agriculture) and Mexico (whose preferential access to the United States is still eroded, because NAFTA is a reciprocal agreement).

Different Behavioral Parameters: Trade Elasticities

The utilization of LINKAGE trade elasticities instead of GTAP elasticities has a very positive impact on trade: for example, under full trade liberalization, international trade of agricultural products is augmented by 57 percent with LINKAGE compared to 34 percent with GTAP trade elasticities. Consequently, the rate of increase in world welfare is 0.44 percent versus 0.33 percent in the central experiment (world welfare gains depend directly on trade increase).

Is this beneficial for developing countries? Yes, because all developing zones benefit from a higher welfare gain except Tunisia, whose welfare increases by 0.3 percent instead of 0.4 percent. The gain is impressive for Rest of Sub-Saharan Africa, Rest of Middle East and North Africa, and Zambia (Figure 4.10).

Figure 4.10   Welfare gains by region: Full trade liberalization with LINKAGE trade elasticities

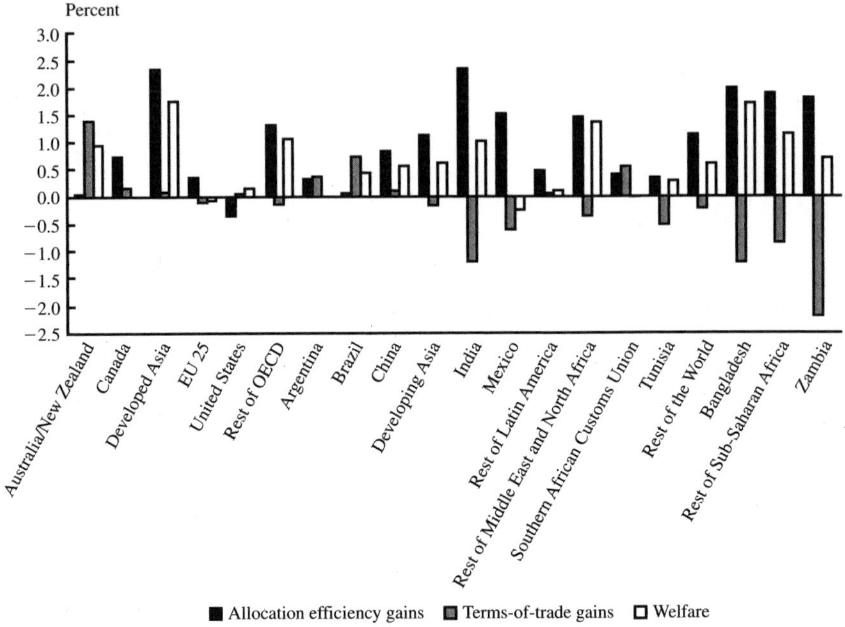

■ Allocation efficiency gains   ■ Terms-of-trade gains   □ Welfare

Different Modeling Features: Trade and Global Factor Productivity

As discussed in the previous section, trade openness may have a positive impact on total factor productivity. This relation can be presented in a simplistic way in a CGEM. Equation (26) is used in this case, which links directly total factor productivity in a sector to the ratio between sector exports and sector output. The relation is implemented in MIRAGE for all sectors and countries. The constant elasticity, relating global factor productivity to the ratio between exports and output, is fixed at 0.055, which is comparable to LINKAGE's elasticity but less than the one adopted by Dessus, Fukasaku, and Safadi (1999). This relation is equally applied to all sectors, agriculture included: Martin and Mitra (2001) show that the relation is even higher in agriculture.

With this relation between trade openness and total factor productivity, expected benefits of full trade liberalization are much amplified, even more than those resulting from the other three sensitivity analyses. The gain in world welfare is now 0.59 percent (Figure 4.11), which represents an augmentation by nearly 80 percent compared to the central experiment.

Figure 4.11   Welfare gains by region: Full trade liberalization using a positive relation between trade openness and total factor productivity

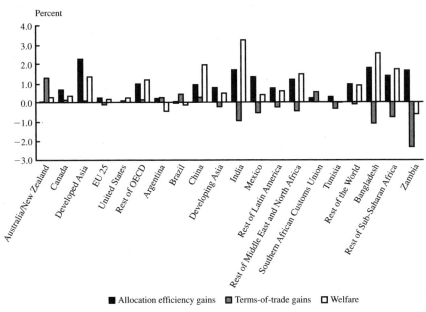

■ Allocation efficiency gains   ■ Terms-of-trade gains   □ Welfare

The issue remains of how liberalization benefits are distributed. Compared to the central experiment, the welfare change is smaller for Argentina, Australia/New Zealand, and Brazil (the loss is larger in the Argentinean case, whereas Brazil has a small loss instead of a small gain); Bangladesh, China, India, Mexico, and Rest of Sub-Saharan Africa exhibit higher rates of growth.

In this matter, agricultural countries can clearly be distinguished from industrial countries. Agricultural specialization is costly because of the absence of economies of scale and horizontal differentiation in this sector: when trade is liberalized, an agricultural country (such as Argentina, Australia, or New Zealand) shows decreased activity in industrial sectors compared to the baseline, which means fewer economies of scale and less horizontal differentiation. The positive relation linking openness and factor productivity amplifies the opportunity cost. In these three agricultural countries, under full trade liberalization, the ratio exports on output calculated at the sector level increases more in agricultural sectors, thus amplifying country specialization in this activity stemming from increased factor productivity and higher competitiveness. The global disengagement of these economies from industry is more pronounced, and the opportunity cost in terms of economies of scale and variety of product is higher. The opposite process works in countries whose comparative advantage is in industry: it explains the higher welfare gains seen for Bangladesh, China, India, and Rest of Sub-Saharan Africa.

Different Modeling Features: Other Choices

As a multicountry, multisector trade model requires numerous theoretical choices, this sensitivity analysis might be extended much further. I limit this extension, however, to three theoretical variations (Table 4.4). The first implements perfect competition in industry and services instead of imperfect competition; the second eliminates the North/South distinction in the model (that is, the vertical differentiation); the third assumes perfect mobility of unskilled labor between agricultural and industrial activities.

Whereas the last two sensitivity analyses do not change the picture, the assumption of perfect competition increases substantially the rate of change in world

Table 4.4   World welfare gains by zone: Full trade liberalization using different theoretical variations (percent)

Country/zone	Central model	Perfect competition	No vertical differentiation	Perfect labor mobility
World	**0.33**	**0.44**	**0.31**	**0.33**
Australia/New Zealand	0.9	1.4	0.8	0.7
Canada	−0.1	0.0	0.0	−0.1
Developed Asia	1.4	1.4	1.4	1.5
EU 25	−0.1	0.1	−0.1	−0.1
Rest of OECD	1.0	0.8	1.1	1.1
United States	0.1	0.2	0.1	0.1
Argentina	−0.1	1.0	−0.3	−0.2
Brazil	0.2	0.9	0.1	0.1
China	0.6	−0.2	0.8	0.7
Developing Asia	0.4	0.5	0.3	0.4
India	0.7	0.4	0.6	0.7
Mexico	−0.3	0.3	−0.4	−0.3
Rest of Latin America	0.0	0.6	−0.1	0.0
Rest of Middle East and North Africa	0.9	0.7	0.9	1.0
Rest of the World	0.1	1.1	0.0	0.2
Southern African Customs Union	−0.2	0.5	−0.2	−0.3
Tunisia	0.4	0.1	0.4	0.4
Bangladesh	1.5	1.3	1.5	1.6
Rest of Sub-Saharan Africa	0.6	0.9	0.6	0.7
Zambia	0.3	−1.2	0.5	0.4

Note: OECD, Organisation for Economic Co-operation and Development.

welfare (from 0.33 percent up to 0.44 percent). Furthermore, the distribution of the pie is modified. In fact, under imperfect competition in industry and services, world real income appears to move upward for 10 years, both in the baseline scenario and for full trade liberalization. Perfect competition in the baseline scenario, however, pulls down to a larger extent the world economy's path, as it is more specialized in industry. Adopting full trade liberalization implies more productive factors in the agricultural activity at the worldwide level, because initially this activity is more protected than industry is. Therefore, the opportunity cost of perfect competition in all sectors is smaller.

As far as the distribution of welfare gains among countries and/or zones is concerned, the picture is fairly unchanged in the last two simulations, but not for perfect competition. As expected, the change in the theoretical features of the model implies more welfare gains for zones with an initial comparative advantage in agriculture (such as Argentina, Australia/New Zealand, Brazil, Rest of Latin America, and SACU) and less welfare gains for countries specializing in industry (including Bangladesh, China, India, and Tunisia).

For Canada, Mexico, and Rest of Sub-Saharan Africa, eroded preferences contribute to a contraction of both agricultural and industrial activities, which were particularly negative in case of imperfect competition. Therefore, when competition is perfect, the erosion of preferences entails fewer negative consequences.

Chapter 5

Conclusions

Recent studies have noted lower expectations regarding the potential impact of trade liberalization on development (see Ackerman 2005; Piermartini and Teh 2005). These reduced forecasts are due to improved assessments of existing trade distortions. Regional agreements, preferential schemes, and recent policy changes in trade and agricultural policies make for a more globalized world than was previously thought. Furthermore, fewer benefits stemming from a potential DDA are expected, as assessments take into account the interplay between bound and applied distortions (on tariffs and domestic support).

Nevertheless, the expected effects from trade liberalization are positive, if very small. My assessment concludes that a gain of US$100 billion in world welfare would occur, mainly as a result of elimination of agricultural distortions. This welfare gain could be amplified by up to 80 percent if openness increases factor productivity. At the same time, liberalization should generally contribute to poverty alleviation, because remuneration of unskilled labor is expected to rise in numerous developing countries, especially in South America, Sub-Saharan Africa, and Developing Asia. Finally, liberalization may only marginally reduce inequality among countries.

This assessment, however, underestimates the positive impact of trade liberalization on world welfare for two reasons:

- It does not include liberalization in services.
- It does not include trade facilitation and elimination of some nontariff barriers (technical, sanitary, and phytosanitary norms).

One of the major objectives of this study was to explain divergent results in the literature. The first explanation comes from different assessments of the current level of trade distortions: it is now widely recognized that these assessments have to take into account preferential schemes and regional agreements. By doing so, assessments have begun to converge, but not fully.

Today, the main source of divergence is the level of trade elasticities and the implementation of dynamic relations. There is no consensus yet on the magnitude of behavioral parameters. Moreover, the link between openness and factor productivity might be strong, but it is not fully understood or precisely estimated.

To understand the impact of nontariff barriers or the nature of dynamic relation, shortcuts are possible: one can evaluate the impact of trade facilitation by assuming that border controls and administrative rules are equivalent to an x percent tariff. One can also suppose that trade openness increases global factor productivity. These options automatically amplify expected benefits from trade liberalization, but they do not improve understanding of the impact of globalization. Furthermore, there may appear benefits from liberalization in areas or activities where they do not now exist. For example, implementing a positive relation between trade openness and global factor productivity could generate very positive results in all developing countries; nevertheless, the strength of this relation is questionable in some LDCs. Capturing the technical progress incorporated in goods requires machinery, skill, and competence. In addition, trade openness may have much greater effects on capital and skilled labor productivity than on unskilled labor; if so, the introduction of this relation could introduce a systematic bias in the assessment of the impact of trade liberalization on poverty.

It could be argued that all CGEMs are structurally identical (they are all Walrassian models), and that their proliferation is not necessary. From the methodological conclusions outlined here, however (convergence on market access data and divergence on trade elasticities, dynamic relations, understanding of trade in services, and nontariff barriers), it appears that on the contrary, CGEMs have to remain competitive. If knowledge about market access has recently increased, it was due to competition among research teams. In this respect, one can expect future progress in the understanding of dynamic relations, trade in services, the impact of nontariff barriers, and so forth.

IFPRI has a role to play by providing consistent analysis of international trade and trade negotiations and agreements. As a nonlending institution, its role could appear especially credible for developing countries. Multicountry CGEMs are only one analytical instrument, one particularly appropriate for assessing the impact of multilateral or regional agreements on trade flows and macroeconomic variables. A complete evaluation of the benefits of trade reform for developing countries requires the addition of other instruments, such as single-country trade models that allow for microsimulations aimed at evaluating the precise impact of trade liberalization on income distribution, partial equilibrium global trade models (such as IMPACT), the gravity equation, and so forth. These are complementary tools, not substitutes—IFPRI also needs to maintain an expertise in these fields.

In terms of policy recommendations, trade reform must be very ambitious to improve welfare and have a positive impact on development. The DDA will not entail an implementation of full trade liberalization. On the contrary, it will lead to a more-or-less ambitious package; recent assessments of trade liberalization scenarios by CGEMs have been successful in showing that the "devil could be in the details." Several policy recommendations emerge clearly from these studies:

1. Tariff cuts have to be large and "progressive" (higher rates of reduction on higher tariffs). On the tariff issue, a sensitive products clause could have highly negative consequences on the extent of liberalization, even if it concerns a limited number of products. Furthermore, implementing a cap on tariffs, even at a relatively high level (200 percent), could be a measure fostering liberalization.
2. Agriculture is the main area where distortions have to be reduced.
3. Developing countries have to liberalize their own economies. The SDT that the WTO offers gives these countries flexibility, but it may have negative consequences on them, because it reduces pressure for critical domestic reforms.

From this modeling exercise and recent studies in the literature, it appears that expected benefits from trade liberalization are surprisingly low. In fact, the consequences of trade liberalization for world real income are modest, because rich countries compose a major part of this income, and they are already close to free trade. Trade liberalization may have a more substantial impact on developing countries. Of course, by comparison, the Asian miracle, Chile's experience, and Chinese and Indian liberalization all brought high growth rates per year, whereas CGEM results show an increase of less than 3 percent in total real income. This disparity could mean either that dynamic gains are not well captured by global trade modeling or that these gains come from the domestic reform accompanying trade liberalization. Furthermore, the consequences of liberalization in the services sector have to be better understood.

These conclusions define five priorities in the research agenda:

1. a better understanding and inclusion of nontariffs barriers, administrative controls, and lack of infrastructure;
2. a better understanding of trade and trade barriers in services;
3. a better understanding of dynamic relations and the way in which trade liberalization affects factor productivity and capital accumulation;

4. knowledge of the nature and the exact content of domestic reforms that could amplify expected benefits from trade liberalization; and
5. a detailed examination of the link between trade and poverty.

For the fifth priority, although the effects of liberalization on average national product and factor prices are quite well established, there is still limited knowledge on price transmission and consumption decisions at the microeconomic level. Researchers have made important progress on this fifth priority in recent years, which is particularly significant, because poverty alleviation remains the ultimate objective of this debate.

Arable Land per Person, by Country

Table A.1   Arable land per person, 2003 (hectares per person)

Country	Arable land	Country	Arable land
Australia	2.40	Uruguay	0.40
Kazakhstan	1.51	Chad	0.39
Canada	1.44	Burkina Faso	0.39
Niger	1.11	Cameroon	0.38
Russian Federation	0.85	New Zealand	0.37
Lithuania	0.85	Mali	0.37
Latvia	0.78	Nicaragua	0.37
Argentina	0.73	Bolivia	0.35
Ukraine	0.68	Benin	0.33
Guyana	0.64	Turkey	0.33
United States	0.60	Poland	0.33
Belarus	0.56	Samoa	0.33
Paraguay	0.52	Croatia	0.33
Central African Republic	0.49	Spain	0.33
Sudan	0.49	Brazil	0.33
Mongolia	0.48	Libya	0.32
Turkmenistan	0.47	South Africa	0.32
Zambia	0.47	France	0.31
Hungary	0.46	Czech Republic	0.30
Moldova	0.44	Sweden	0.30
Romania	0.43	Ireland	0.30
Togo	0.43	Morocco	0.29
Bulgaria	0.42	Afghanistan	0.29
Finland	0.42	Tunisia	0.28
Denmark	0.42	Macedonia, Former	
Serbia and Montenegro	0.42	Yugoslavian Republic	0.28
Namibia	0.41	Cambodia	0.27
Estonia	0.40	Cuba	0.27

(continued)

Country	Arable land	Country	Arable land
Equatorial Guinea	0.27	Burundi	0.14
Kyrgyz Republic	0.26	Timor-Leste	0.14
Bosnia and Herzegovina	0.26	Comoros	0.14
Belize	0.26	Eritrea	0.14
Syrian Arab Republic	0.25	Italy	0.14
Zimbabwe	0.25	Rwanda	0.14
Greece	0.24	Peru	0.14
Islamic Republic of Iran	0.24	Somalia	0.14
Mexico	0.24	Republic of Congo	0.13
Gabon	0.24	Pakistan	0.13
Nigeria	0.24	Suriname	0.13
Fiji	0.24	Dominican Republic	0.13
Algeria	0.24	Ecuador	0.13
Mozambique	0.23	Chile	0.12
Thailand	0.22	Bhutan	0.12
Senegal	0.22	Democratic Republic of Congo	0.12
Angola	0.22	Cyprus	0.12
The Gambia	0.22	Guinea	0.12
Azerbaijan	0.22	Democratic Republic of Korea	0.12
Botswana	0.21	Guatemala	0.12
Iraq	0.21	Liberia	0.12
Myanmar	0.20	Liechtenstein	0.12
Guinea-Bissau	0.20	Sierra Leone	0.11
Malawi	0.20	China	0.11
Ghana	0.20	Tanzania	0.11
Uganda	0.19	Venezuela	0.10
Norway	0.19	Antigua and Barbuda	0.10
Côte d'Ivoire	0.19	El Salvador	0.10
Albania	0.19	Vanuatu	0.10
Lesotho	0.18	Indonesia	0.10
Uzbekistan	0.18	Cape Verde	0.10
Georgia	0.18	United Kingdom	0.09
Panama	0.18	Haiti	0.09
Austria	0.17	Nepal	0.09
Mauritania	0.17	Slovenia	0.09
Laos People's Democratic Republic	0.17	Belgium	0.08
		Vietnam	0.08
Madagascar	0.17	Mauritius	0.08
Armenia	0.16	Republic of Yemen	0.08
Ethiopia	0.16	Malaysia	0.07
Swaziland	0.16	Philippines	0.07
Honduras	0.15	Dominica	0.07
Saudi Arabia	0.15	Jamaica	0.07
Portugal	0.15	Faeroe Islands	0.06
India	0.15	Barbados	0.06
St. Kitts and Nevis	0.15	St. Vincent and the Grenadines	0.06
Tonga	0.15	Bangladesh	0.06
Tajikistan	0.15	Trinidad and Tobago	0.06
Germany	0.14	Netherlands	0.06
Kenya	0.14	Switzerland	0.06

Country	Arable land	Country	Arable land
Jordan	0.06	St. Lucia	0.02
Costa Rica	0.05	Qatar	0.02
São Tomé and Príncipe	0.05	Iceland	0.02
Colombia	0.05	Cayman Islands	0.02
Israel	0.05	Kiribati	0.02
Lebanon	0.05	Aruba	0.02
Sri Lanka	0.05	Grenada	0.02
Netherlands Antilles	0.04	Virgin Islands (U.S.)	0.02
Arab Republic of Egypt	0.04	United Arab Emirates	0.02
Papua New Guinea	0.04	Bermuda	0.02
Solomon Islands	0.04	Andorra	0.02
Federal States of Micronesia	0.04	Oman	0.01
San Marino	0.04	Maldives	0.01
American Samoa	0.04	Guam	0.01
Japan	0.03	Seychelles	0.01
Republic of Korea	0.03	French Polynesia	0.01
Marshall Islands	0.03	Puerto Rico	0.01
Brunei	0.03	Kuwait	0.01
New Caledonia	0.03	Bahrain	0.00
The Bahamas	0.03	Djibouti	0.00
Malta	0.03	Singapore	0.00

Source: World Bank (2003).

Correspondence Tables

Table B.1 Correspondence, sector

GTAP code	Label	Aggregation code
pdr	Paddy rice	Otag
wht	Wheat	Whet
gro	Cereal grains nec	Otag
v_f	Vegetables, fruits, and nuts	VgFr
osd	Oil seeds	Otag
c_b	Sugar cane and sugar beet	Otag
pfb	Plant-based fibers	Plfb
ocr	Crops nec	Otag
ctl	Cattle, sheep, goats, and horses	Meat
oap	Animal products nec	Meat
rmk	Raw milk	Otag
wol	Wool, silkworm cocoons	Oprm
frs	Forestry	Oprm
fsh	Fishing	Oprm
coa	Coal	Oprm
oil	Oil	Oprm
gas	Gas	Oprm
omn	Minerals nec	Oprm
cmt	Meat: cattle, sheep, goat, horse	Meat
omt	Meat products nec	OtFP
vol	Vegetable oils and fats	OtFP
mil	Dairy products	Milk
pcr	Processed rice	Rice
sgr	Sugar	Sugr
ofd	Food products nec	OtFP
b_t	Beverages and tobacco products	OtFP
tex	Textiles	Text
wap	Wearing apparel	Weap

(continued)

GTAP code	Label	Aggregation code
lea	Leather products	Weap
lum	Wood products	Omnf
ppp	Paper products and publishing	Omnf
p_c	Petroleum and coal products	Mich
crp	Chemical, rubber, and plastic products	Mich
nmm	Mineral products nec	Mich
i_s	Ferrous metals	Mich
nfm	Metals nec	Mich
fmp	Metal products	Mich
mvh	Motor vehicles and parts	Veeq
otn	Transport equipment nec	Veeq
ele	Electronic equipment	Veeq
ome	Machinery and equipment nec	Veeq
omf	Manufactures nec	Omnf
ely	Electricity	Omnf
gdt	Gas manufacture and distribution	Omnf
wtr	Water	OtSr
cns	Construction	OtSr
trd	Trade	TrT
otp	Transport nec	TrT
wtp	Sea transport	TrT
atp	Air transport	TrT
cmn	Communication	OtSr
ofi	Financial services nec	OtSr
isr	Insurance	OtSr
obs	Business services nec	OtSr
ros	Recreation and other services	OtSr
osg	Public administration, defense, health, and education	OtSr
dwe	Dwellings	OtSr
aus	Australia	AUNZ
nzl	New Zealand	AUNZ
xoc	Rest of Oceania	RofW
chn	China	Chin
hkg	Hong Kong	DvdA
jpn	Japan	DvdA
kor	Korea	DvdA
twn	Taiwan	DvdA
xea	Rest of East Asia	DvgA
idn	Indonesia	DvgA
mys	Malaysia	DvgA
phl	Philippines	DvgA
sgp	Singapore	DvgA
tha	Thailand	DvgA
vnm	Vietnam	DvgA
xse	Rest of Southeast Asia	DvgA
bgd	Bangladesh	Bgld
ind	India	Indi
lka	Sri Lanka	DvgA
xsa	Rest of South Asia	DvgA
can	Canada	Cana

GTAP code	Label	Aggregation code
usa	United States	USAm
mex	Mexico	Mexi
xna	Rest of Latin America	Rame
col	Colombia	Rame
per	Peru	Rame
ven	Venezuela	Rame
xap	Rest of Andean Pact	Rame
arg	Argentina	Arge

Note: GTAP, Global Trade Analysis Project; nec, not elsewhere classified.

Table B.2   Correspondence, country/zone

GTAP code	Label	Aggregation code
bra	Brazil	Braz
chl	Chile	Rame
ury	Uruguay	Rame
xsm	Rest of Latin America	Rame
xca	Central America	Rame
xfa	Rest of FTAA	Rame
xcb	Rest of the Caribbean	Rame
aut	Austria	EU25
bel	Belgium	EU25
dnk	Denmark	EU25
fin	Finland	EU25
fra	France	EU25
deu	Germany	EU25
gbr	United Kingdom	EU25
grc	Greece	EU25
irl	Ireland	EU25
ita	Italy	EU25
lux	Luxembourg	EU25
nld	Netherlands	EU25
prt	Portugal	EU25
esp	Spain	EU25
swe	Sweden	EU25
che	Switzerland	Roec
xef	Rest of EFTA	Roec
xer	Rest of Europe	Roec
alb	Albania	RofW
bgr	Bulgaria	RofW
hrv	Croatia	RofW
cyp	Cyprus	EU25
cze	Czech Republic	EU25

(continued)

GTAP code	Label	Aggregation code
hun	Hungary	EU25
mlt	Malta	EU25
pol	Poland	EU25
rom	Romania	RofW
svk	Slovakia	EU25
svn	Slovenia	EU25
est	Estonia	EU25
lva	Latvia	EU25
ltu	Lithuania	EU25
rus	Russian Federation	RofW
xsu	Rest of Former Soviet Union	RofW
tur	Turkey	Rmen
xme	Rest of Middle East	Rmen
mar	Morocco	Rmen
tun	Tunisia	Tuni
xnf	Rest of North Africa	Rmen
bwa	Botswana	RSSA
zaf	South Africa	SACU
xsc	Rest of Southern African Customs Union	SACU
mwi	Malawi	RSSA
moz	Mozambique	RSSA
tza	Tanzania	RSSA
zmb	Zambia	Zamb
zwe	Zimbabwe	RSSA
xsd	Rest of SADC	RSSA
mdg	Madagascar	RSSA
uga	Uganda	RSSA
xss	Rest of Sub-Saharan Africa	RSSA

Notes: EFTA, European Free Trade Area; FTAA, Free Trade Area of the Americas; GTAP, Global Trade Analysis Project; SADC, Southern African Development Community.

Initial Patterns of World Trade

Table C.1   Initial pattern of protection, by trade partner, 2005 (level of tariff, percent)

	Australia/ New Zealand	Canada	Developed Asia	EU 25	Rest of OECD	United States	Argentina	Brazil	China
Australia/New Zealand	1.2	3.5	5.2	5.3	2.8	3.1	2.2	3.0	6.0
Canada	6.7	n.a.	2.9	4.6	2.2	0.5	2.1	4.3	4.8
Developed Asia	9.2	5.2	4.0	5.3	2.6	4.6	13.5	11.1	4.4
EU 25	10.8	4.6	3.5	n.a.	0.4	3.5	6.4	6.9	4.0
Rest of OECD	23.2	6.3	1.4	4.6	0.7	5.7	17.5	13.9	2.2
United States	2.4	0.1	2.1	2.7	1.4	n.a.	3.4	2.9	4.4
Argentina	11.7	12.5	13.4	13.7	11.4	13.2	n.a.	4.7	15.4
Brazil	9.7	8.8	13.9	13.9	9.4	10.6	3.3	n.a.	15.2
China	7.4	5.5	8.7	8.3	7.0	5.8	7.9	8.6	n.a.
Developing Asia	7.0	3.5	7.4	5.7	2.8	7.8	11.1	14.7	6.4
India	34.0	37.2	31.8	30.5	32.8	28.5	48.1	34.2	33.8
Mexico	17.9	1.6	13.1	17.0	11.9	1.1	18.9	24.4	21.3
Rest of Latin America	9.8	13.4	8.6	10.5	11.3	8.0	9.2	10.1	11.2
Rest of MENA	14.0	6.0	9.4	7.5	5.7	9.6	14.8	13.7	13.6
Rest of the World	12.6	11.3	8.1	8.6	7.9	9.5	12.2	13.0	11.8
SACU	16.3	9.9	7.0	8.1	3.3	7.9	8.8	17.2	12.2
Bangladesh	10.7	10.1	19.0	14.9	7.4	15.8	17.3	19.2	20.5
Rest of Sub-Saharan Africa	11.6	14.2	13.0	16.3	12.2	15.6	16.5	20.4	21.9
Zambia	7.6	8.2	15.1	11.6	11.0	7.2	8.3	18.9	13.8
Average	9.7	3.9	5.4	5.6	2.4	5.2	10.5	10.1	5.6

Source: Author's calculations using MacMap-HS6.

Notes: Importing countries are listed in rows, exporting countries in columns. Diagonal values indicate inter-zone protection. MENA, Middle East and North Africa; SACU, Southern African Customs Union.

Developing Asia	India	Mexico	Rest of Latin America	Rest of MENA	Rest of the World	SACU	Bangladesh	Rest of Sub-Saharan Africa	Zambia	Average
3.5	7.5	6.6	4.7	5.1	3.7	4.1	15.1	3.6	0.3	4.8
2.7	5.8	0.2	2.8	2.1	2.0	1.9	14.3	0.8	0.2	3.4
4.3	10.6	4.4	6.6	3.2	4.0	5.0	3.9	4.0	1.9	4.9
3.0	5.4	1.4	5.1	0.6	1.3	3.0	0.0	1.3	1.1	3.2
2.6	5.2	5.1	6.2	1.9	3.5	3.9	0.4	2.0	1.7	4.3
2.3	4.4	0.0	2.3	1.5	1.6	0.8	11.4	1.0	0.9	2.3
11.2	13.9	9.7	8.1	8.3	10.9	13.0	16.0	5.6	10.6	12.5
11.0	11.6	13.4	9.8	6.0	7.3	11.8	13.5	2.4	7.5	11.8
7.2	7.8	7.7	7.7	5.2	7.7	7.8	7.3	2.8	2.9	7.6
5.4	9.2	3.9	8.3	4.4	6.9	8.6	2.7	6.8	6.5	6.5
35.7	n.a.	27.9	31.2	28.0	31.7	34.6	13.2	22.8	34.4	31.8
12.2	20.8	n.a.	7.4	14.1	17.8	16.9	24.7	14.9	14.5	10.8
8.7	9.8	15.1	9.6	12.9	8.6	9.3	12.2	10.9	6.9	9.6
9.7	14.4	8.3	14.7	7.2	9.8	12.8	19.5	8.5	9.1	9.2
8.2	10.4	9.3	11.1	7.2	4.7	12.3	10.0	5.0	6.0	8.9
5.9	13.4	6.2	11.3	6.1	8.0	0.0	16.8	3.3	3.3	8.2
19.8	17.2	27.2	25.4	17.0	15.4	12.1	n.a.	29.0	17.5	17.4
20.6	20.9	13.8	14.9	17.4	12.6	19.5	18.7	18.7	12.6	16.9
14.9	10.7	15.1	10.6	11.3	9.5	11.5	23.7	6.5	n.a.	11.8
5.1	8.3	2.2	6.6	3.0	4.9	7.7	4.9	4.4	4.7	n.a.

Table C.2   Initial pattern of protection, by product, 2005 (level of tariff, percent)

	Meat: cattle, sheep, goat, horse	Milk (processed)	Plant-based fibers	Rice (processed)	Sugar (processed)	Vegetables and fruit	Wheat
Australia/New Zealand	0.0	0.9	0.0	0.0	2.1	0.5	0.0
Canada	7.9	103.2	0.0	0.0	3.7	2.1	1.7
Developed Asia	21.5	46.1	0.2	614.7	139.5	18.4	79.8
EU 25	39.7	47.0	0.0	138.6	128.6	17.9	0.5
Rest of OECD	102.3	88.1	0.0	13.3	44.0	31.5	108.4
United States	1.7	18.8	1.6	4.9	34.9	2.7	2.4
Argentina	8.6	16.8	7.4	12.2	17.5	10.4	5.7
Brazil	6.0	19.7	8.8	14.5	17.5	8.8	4.6
China	9.9	11.4	1.1	1.0	19.8	11.9	1.0
Developing Asia	3.8	5.5	1.6	16.8	19.4	10.1	7.7
India	24.2	51.4	5.6	72.8	59.5	41.4	100.0
Mexico	14.3	32.6	5.2	17.4	20.8	22.8	28.2
Rest of Latin America	10.3	19.2	5.1	31.2	29.4	14.1	5.9
Rest of Middle East and North Africa	26.4	40.8	3.7	19.3	30.7	26.7	17.1
Rest of the World	14.5	27.4	1.1	9.6	36.5	20.3	22.8
Southern African Customs Union	12.5	38.3	13.5	0.0	97.3	7.3	36.3
Bangladesh	17.7	34.8	0.2	5.0	25.2	16.8	5.0
Rest of Sub-Saharan Africa	16.9	19.7	6.1	32.1	23.1	32.3	10.6
Zambia	9.3	13.8	5.5	4.9	23.7	16.7	5.0
Average	21.4	33.1	2.3	71.9	52.2	14.2	16.1

Source: Author's calculations using MacMap-HS6.
Note: OECD, Organisation for Economic Co-operation and Development.

Other agricultural products	Other food products	Other primary products	Textile	Wearing apparel	Metal, mineral, petroleum, and chemical products	Vehicles and equipment	Other manufacturing products	Average
0.1	3.9	3.2	12.7	16.8	3.0	4.9	3.4	4.8
1.1	10.9	0.1	10.4	13.5	2.0	1.7	1.5	3.4
38.3	15.8	1.6	6.0	8.7	2.5	3.1	1.5	4.9
7.5	11.1	0.1	5.8	7.1	2.1	2.2	1.0	3.2
32.9	37.0	0.2	3.6	2.7	0.7	0.5	1.1	4.3
2.8	3.7	0.0	9.0	10.9	2.1	1.3	0.6	2.3
7.4	14.1	0.8	18.3	19.7	12.1	12.8	13.7	12.5
6.7	13.3	0.8	18.1	18.2	10.7	13.4	12.5	11.8
11.1	15.5	1.2	11.3	13.2	7.9	7.3	5.4	7.6
20.5	12.1	1.4	10.3	7.5	5.8	6.4	5.6	6.5
46.1	63.1	19.5	29.4	32.7	32.4	25.3	27.4	31.8
29.5	29.9	10.3	14.5	24.0	9.3	7.7	10.6	10.8
8.4	16.5	13.2	11.7	14.5	8.1	8.4	10.0	9.6
18.2	21.7	4.8	14.3	25.6	7.4	6.8	8.6	9.2
7.5	23.4	2.5	11.0	16.3	7.9	7.4	10.1	8.9
9.6	14.3	0.3	21.5	31.3	5.4	6.2	8.0	8.2
15.9	26.5	22.0	29.7	28.7	16.8	11.8	21.8	17.4
20.5	33.4	7.1	29.4	36.0	15.4	12.1	19.9	16.9
8.0	19.0	7.3	16.5	24.4	8.6	11.0	16.2	11.8
14.5	13.9	1.3	9.5	10.3	4.4	3.8	2.9	

Table C.3   Initial pattern of trade, by importing country, 2005 (percent)

	Australia/ New Zealand	Canada	Developed Asia	EU 25	Rest of OECD	United States	Argentina	Brazil	China
Australia/New Zealand	5.8	2.0	28.2	19.2	0.9	12.2	0.2	0.5	6.6
Canada	0.5	0.0	4.9	10.5	0.7	74.6	0.1	0.4	1.8
Developed Asia	1.8	2.0	14.6	19.0	0.9	25.3	0.2	0.8	13.4
EU 25	0.9	1.4	5.3	59.7	4.0	11.2	0.3	0.9	1.8
Rest of OECD	0.8	2.0	6.4	60.2	1.2	12.8	0.2	0.8	1.5
United States	1.8	16.2	15.2	30.3	1.6	0.0	0.6	1.9	3.3
Argentina	0.5	1.1	4.4	21.8	0.7	10.7	0.0	19.9	4.4
Brazil	0.5	1.5	7.6	28.7	1.3	23.3	7.4	0.0	3.6
China	1.7	2.2	30.4	20.0	0.7	28.5	0.3	0.4	0.0
Developing Asia	2.1	1.3	21.1	20.5	0.7	19.7	0.2	0.5	6.4
India	1.1	1.7	9.3	29.6	1.3	19.9	0.3	1.4	3.5
Mexico	0.3	3.3	2.2	6.9	0.4	78.6	0.3	0.5	0.7
Rest of Latin America	0.5	2.8	7.2	22.7	1.9	33.1	1.1	2.8	2.1
Rest of MENA	0.8	0.9	20.2	31.8	0.9	17.5	0.2	1.0	3.1
Rest of the World	0.6	0.5	5.3	44.0	3.6	7.1	0.1	0.5	5.6
SACU	1.3	0.9	10.6	36.5	1.6	12.5	0.2	1.0	2.7
Tunisia	0.5	0.8	3.1	71.5	1.0	6.4	0.3	0.5	0.9
Bangladesh	0.5	1.8	4.0	44.3	1.2	37.4	0.1	0.4	0.2
Rest of Sub-Saharan Africa	0.3	0.7	6.1	40.7	1.4	25.5	0.2	2.5	4.2
Zambia	0.1	0.1	8.6	45.9	3.9	1.6	0.0	0.1	3.2

Source: Author's calculations using MacMap-HS6.

Notes: Importing countries are listed in columns, exporting countries in rows. MENA, Middle East and North Africa; OECD, Organisation for Economic Co-operation and Development; SACU, Southern African Customs Union.

Developing Asia	India	Mexico	Rest of Latin America	Rest of MENA	SACU	Tunisia	Bangladesh	Rest of Sub-Saharan Africa	Zambia	Rest of the World	Total
10.4	1.7	0.9	1.2	6.0	0.9	0.0	0.3	0.7	0.0	2.3	100.0
1.3	0.3	1.1	1.7	1.3	0.1	0.0	0.0	0.3	0.0	0.5	100.0
12.0	0.7	1.2	2.4	3.5	0.4	0.0	0.2	0.8	0.0	0.9	100.0
2.6	0.6	0.8	1.3	4.4	0.5	0.3	0.0	1.0	0.0	2.9	100.0
3.2	0.5	0.8	1.6	5.0	0.3	0.1	0.1	0.7	0.0	1.8	100.0
6.1	0.7	10.2	4.6	4.7	0.5	0.1	0.1	0.8	0.0	1.4	100.0
3.8	1.8	1.6	17.8	7.4	1.1	0.3	0.8	0.9	0.0	1.0	100.0
2.7	0.6	3.0	10.0	5.1	0.7	0.1	0.2	1.1	0.0	2.5	100.0
6.6	0.7	0.8	1.7	2.9	0.3	0.0	0.3	1.0	0.0	1.3	100.0
18.2	1.9	0.9	0.9	3.1	0.3	0.0	0.4	0.9	0.0	0.8	100.0
9.9	0.0	0.7	1.4	10.8	0.7	0.1	2.0	3.7	0.0	2.6	100.0
0.8	0.9	0.0	4.1	0.5	0.1	0.0	0.0	0.1	0.0	0.3	100.0
1.9	2.8	2.7	14.6	1.6	0.2	0.0	0.0	0.4	0.0	1.5	100.0
7.6	2.2	0.4	0.7	8.9	0.5	0.2	0.2	1.0	0.0	1.9	100.0
2.1	0.7	0.3	1.5	7.0	0.1	0.1	0.1	0.6	0.0	20.2	100.0
2.7	3.3	0.7	0.8	4.5	9.9	0.0	0.0	8.1	1.3	1.3	100.0
1.5	1.2	0.4	0.9	8.6	0.2	0.0	0.2	1.1	0.0	1.1	100.0
3.2	0.8	0.4	0.6	4.2	0.1	0.0	0.0	0.5	0.0	0.4	100.0
2.9	1.4	0.4	1.1	2.3	3.5	0.1	0.1	5.1	0.2	1.2	100.0
6.6	1.1	0.1	0.2	9.6	12.3	0.0	0.1	5.6	0.0	0.8	100.0

Table C.4   Initial structure of exports, 2005 (percent)

	Australia/ New Zealand	Canada	Developed Asia	EU 25	Rest of OECD	United States	Argentina	Brazil	China
Meat: cattle, sheep, goat, horse	7.7	1.4	0.1	0.6	0.2	0.9	1.3	1.8	0.4
Milk (processed)	5.4	0.2	0.0	0.8	0.3	0.1	1.1	0.1	0.0
Plant-based fibers	1.2	0.0	0.0	0.0	0.0	0.3	0.3	0.2	0.0
Rice (processed)	0.2	0.0	0.0	0.0	0.0	0.1	0.2	0.0	0.2
Sugar (processed)	0.8	0.1	0.0	0.1	0.0	0.0	0.1	2.0	0.0
Vegetables and fruits	1.7	0.5	0.0	0.6	0.0	0.6	2.5	0.6	0.5
Wheat	1.8	1.1	0.0	0.2	0.0	0.4	5.2	0.0	0.0
Other agricultural products	1.3	0.9	0.2	0.6	0.2	2.0	19.5	13.9	0.7
Other food products	5.4	3.2	0.7	4.1	3.2	2.7	18.0	9.2	1.9
Other primary products	19.1	7.3	0.1	1.0	14.4	0.7	8.2	6.2	1.2
Textiles	0.5	0.7	4.8	1.7	0.7	1.3	0.8	1.1	11.9
Wearing apparel	0.8	0.5	1.6	1.8	0.6	0.7	2.4	3.0	29.3
Metal, mineral, petroleum, and chemical products	20.3	17.0	16.7	23.0	26.4	17.2	16.2	18.6	11.3
Vehicles and equipment	10.2	40.2	56.3	38.3	25.5	43.8	10.1	23.4	24.9
Other manufacturing products	4.6	15.0	3.0	7.5	8.0	5.0	3.3	7.8	12.8
Other services	9.1	7.4	6.3	12.5	12.4	17.5	5.9	8.9	1.7
Transport and trade	9.8	4.6	10.4	7.4	8.1	6.9	5.0	3.3	3.1
Total	100.0	100.0	100.0	100.0	100.0	100.0	100.0	100.0	100.0

Source: Author's calculations using MacMap-HS6.
Notes: MENA, Middle East and North Africa; OECD, Organisation for Economic Co-operation and Development; SACU, Southern African Customs Union.

Developing Asia	India	Mexico	Rest of Latin America	Rest of MENA	SACU	Tunisia	Bangladesh	Rest of Sub-Saharan Africa	Zambia	Rest of the World
0.2	0.7	0.3	0.8	0.3	0.9	0.5	0.1	0.7	0.3	0.6
0.1	0.1	0.0	0.3	0.1	0.2	0.2	0.0	0.1	0.0	0.3
0.0	0.1	0.0	0.1	0.2	0.1	0.1	1.2	1.8	1.0	0.6
0.5	1.0	0.0	0.2	0.1	0.1	0.0	0.0	0.1	0.0	0.0
0.2	0.4	0.1	1.2	0.1	1.2	0.1	0.0	0.7	3.0	0.1
0.5	1.2	1.7	4.0	1.3	2.6	1.4	0.3	2.4	0.9	0.3
0.0	0.7	0.1	0.0	0.1	0.1	0.2	0.0	0.0	0.0	0.5
1.5	2.9	0.4	3.6	0.6	1.0	0.4	0.6	8.6	4.2	1.1
4.6	4.2	2.3	8.2	1.7	4.3	4.5	4.9	5.3	0.7	3.1
4.5	2.2	6.9	16.2	40.0	10.6	5.4	0.2	43.6	0.5	27.4
4.1	13.2	2.2	2.6	2.6	1.3	2.8	24.5	1.5	2.2	1.4
4.4	11.9	3.0	4.8	2.8	1.2	14.3	45.4	2.2	0.3	3.1
11.6	20.0	9.8	23.7	19.5	36.7	16.1	7.3	8.4	70.2	34.6
48.2	8.4	62.2	9.3	8.8	14.7	20.6	1.8	3.4	2.3	9.6
6.1	13.3	4.2	6.1	5.2	15.5	2.9	0.7	6.7	11.6	6.0
8.0	12.3	3.4	9.0	8.5	3.1	12.3	11.0	7.7	1.2	5.5
5.7	7.6	3.5	10.1	8.3	6.5	18.2	2.2	7.1	1.8	5.7
100.0	100.0	100.0	100.0	100.0	100.0	100.0	100.0	100.0	100.0	100.0

Impact of Full Trade Liberalization on World Prices

Table D.1 Impact of full trade liberalization on world prices, by sector (percent)

	World	Australia/ New Zealand	Canada	Developed Asia	EU 25	Rest of OECD	United States	Argentina	Brazil
Meat: cattle, sheep, goat, horse	5.9	13.0	6.4	−4.6	4.3	−13.4	3.3	−0.4	16.1
Milk (processed)	4.6	11.6	−2.5	−5.5	4.6	0.5	5.2	3.2	4.2
Plant-based fibers	6.9	9.0	4.2	6.7	24.1	6.7	8.3	5.8	6.6
Rice (processed)	3.0	8.2	4.7	−21.4	−9.7	−2.4	2.1	−6.4	4.9
Sugar (processed)	2.3	11.3	2.0	−18.2	−7.3	−5.2	1.8	−1.2	3.4
Vegetables and fruits	5.3	11.1	8.7	4.0	1.6	−6.5	9.4	5.2	8.2
Wheat	10.6	13.5	9.8	−21.5	10.4	−10.4	15.5	9.9	8.4
Other agricultural products	8.3	16.3	8.6	−9.6	7.9	3.3	14.8	6.3	10.2
Other food products	−0.9	7.8	2.3	−15.1	−1.2	−4.8	2.3	3.3	4.7
Other primary products	2.9	6.4	2.2	2.6	3.0	6.2	2.1	−2.7	2.4
Textiles	3.6	4.2	0.1	2.2	−1.6	−1.7	0.8	−1.6	−1.8
Wearing apparel	3.8	2.5	1.0	2.9	−1.0	−1.0	0.5	−0.8	0.8
Metal, mineral, petroleum, and chemical products	0.3	5.5	1.6	1.2	1.1	0.4	1.5	4.8	0.3
Vehicles and equipment	1.5	4.5	2.1	1.9	4.0	1.3	1.4	4.1	1.1
Other manufacturing products	0.2	5.7	1.3	0.7	−1.2	1.0	1.4	−3.0	3.3
Other services	1.2	5.6	−1.8	4.5	−0.3	0.5	1.4	8.5	6.2
Transport and trade	1.2	5.3	1.1	3.0	0.1	2.2	1.4	−5.2	4.6

Notes: MENA, Middle East and North Africa; OECD, Organisation for Economic Co-operation and Development; SACU, Southern African Customs Union.

China	Developing Asia	India	Mexico	Rest of Latin America	Rest of MENA	Rest of the World	SACU	Tunisia	Bangladesh	Rest of Sub-Saharan Africa	Zambia
7.2	5.0	0.4	2.3	4.0	−6.1	3.3	4.4	3.5	0.8	−1.0	4.3
0.1	0.2	−3.0	−11.7	2.1	−3.3	−0.2	0.2	1.1	−9.8	−6.9	3.5
3.8	6.9	4.5	4.4	5.4	4.5	4.1	1.3	5.1	−5.7	−0.2	4.1
5.9	4.2	5.5	3.0	2.0	2.2	1.5	2.3	−0.6	0.5	0.5	5.7
6.6	−1.3	−3.9	4.5	7.1	0.6	−1.3	4.0	−0.2	−0.7	0.3	7.2
9.6	8.1	−0.1	6.2	7.8	1.6	5.6	6.3	4.3	1.0	2.1	8.5
5.4	10.2	7.2	15.3	5.0	1.1	5.3	5.0	0.4	2.9	7.4	4.9
8.5	6.1	1.4	5.4	5.6	1.0	4.6	4.9	2.9	2.1	2.1	7.5
−4.7	−2.3	−5.5	0.7	0.9	−0.8	0.9	2.7	−0.8	−5.6	−1.6	5.7
4.7	4.3	−6.4	3.8	−1.3	4.4	−0.4	4.7	2.7	−0.3	2.4	5.9
12.4	7.1	0.3	−0.5	0.1	−0.8	1.7	−0.0	−6.2	7.8	−5.0	1.1
10.6	1.8	−3.3	−4.3	−0.7	−1.1	0.6	−2.3	−6.6	−7.2	−5.2	1.6
−2.7	2.4	−7.5	2.2	−0.2	−7.3	1.1	2.8	−0.8	−15.5	−4.9	−6.8
−2.1	−1.5	−7.7	−1.5	0.6	2.3	1.7	2.0	2.1	12.9	−13.6	−17.4
1.5	4.9	−5.2	4.2	0.7	−2.9	1.4	2.4	0.8	−5.9	−1.3	8.4
4.0	5.9	−0.6	7.3	2.8	2.8	5.6	2.3	3.1	2.6	−0.2	9.1
0.2	5.6	−2.7	−9.9	0.7	1.1	4.1	2.3	4.3	2.8	−0.5	9.1

Decomposition of Full Trade Liberalization, by Liberalizing Region

Table E.1   Impact of full trade
liberalization in the North:
Rate of change for world
indicators for 2015 (percent)

Indicator	Total
World agricultural trade	10.81
World trade	−2.37
World welfare	0.11

Table E.2   Impact of full trade liberalization in the North: Rate of change of macroeconomic indicators for 2015 (percent)

Country/zone	Allocation efficiency gains	Terms-of-trade gains	Welfare
Australia/New Zealand	0.1	0.6	0.2
Canada	0.6	0.0	0.0
Developed Asia	2.3	−0.2	1.2
EU 25	0.2	−0.3	−0.2
United States	0.0	−0.1	−0.1
Rest of OECD	1.0	−0.3	0.8
Argentina	−0.1	−0.2	−0.4
Brazil	0.0	0.3	0.3
China	−1.0	1.4	−0.3
Developing Asia	0.0	0.6	0.3
India	−0.1	0.2	0.3
Mexico	−0.2	−0.1	−0.5
Rest of Latin America	0.0	0.4	0.2
Rest of Middle East and North Africa	−0.2	0.2	0.0
Southern African Customs Union	0.0	0.2	−0.2
Tunisia	0.1	−0.1	0.3
Rest of the World	0.0	0.2	0.2
Bangladesh	0.0	0.4	0.8
Rest of Sub-Saharan Africa	0.0	0.1	0.0
Zambia	−0.2	−0.2	−0.7

Note: OECD, Organisation for Economic Co-operation and Development.

Table E.3   Impact of full trade liberalization in the South: Rate of change for world indicators for 2015 (percent)

Indicator	Total
World agricultural trade	18.66
World trade	5.19
World welfare	0.06

Table E.4.   Impact of full trade liberalization in the South: Rate of change of macroeconomic indicators for 2015 (percent)

Country/zone	Allocation efficiency gains	Terms-of-trade gains	Welfare
Australia/New Zealand	0.0	0.8	0.6
Canada	0.0	0.1	–0.2
Developed Asia	0.0	0.2	0.1
EU 25	–0.1	0.2	0.0
United States	0.0	0.1	0.1
Rest of OECD	0.0	0.3	0.1
Argentina	0.2	0.0	–0.5
Brazil	0.1	–0.1	–0.2
China	0.8	–0.2	0.2
Developing Asia	0.7	–0.6	0.0
India	1.5	–1.0	0.5
Mexico	1.3	–0.3	0.0
Rest of Latin America	0.8	–0.6	–0.1
Rest of Middle East and North Africa	1.2	–0.7	0.8
Rest of the World	1.1	–0.5	–0.5
Southern African Customs Union	0.3	0.3	–0.1
Tunisia	0.4	0.0	0.7
Bangladesh	1.8	–1.2	1.4
Rest of Sub-Saharan Africa	1.3	–0.9	0.5
Zambia	1.8	–2.2	1.1

Note: OECD, Organisation for Economic Co-operation and Development.

Decomposition of Full Trade Liberalization, by Activity

Table F.1 Impact of full trade liberalization in agriculture: Rate of change of world indicators for 2015 (percent)

Indicator	Total
World agricultural trade	37.6
World trade	1.6
World welfare	0.18

Table F.2 Impact of full trade liberalization in agriculture: Rate of change of macroeconomic indicators for 2015 (percent)

Country/zone	Allocation efficiency gains	Terms-of-trade gains	Welfare
Australia/New Zealand	−0.1	0.9	0.5
Canada	0.3	0.0	0.1
Developed Asia	2.1	−0.2	1.1
EU 25	0.1	−0.1	0.0
United States	0.0	0.0	−0.1
Rest of OECD	1.0	−0.3	0.8
Argentina	0.0	0.2	0.2
Brazil	0.0	0.6	0.4
China	−0.1	1.0	−0.1
Developing Asia	0.4	0.3	0.0
India	0.7	−0.1	0.6
Mexico	0.3	−0.1	0.0
Rest of Latin America	0.1	0.2	0.1
Rest of Middle East and North Africa	0.4	−0.2	0.2
Southern African Customs Union	0.2	0.2	0.4
Tunisia	0.2	0.2	0.5
Rest of the World	0.3	0.0	0.4
Bangladesh	0.1	0.1	0.7
Rest of Sub-Saharan Africa	0.8	−0.3	0.6
Zambia	0.2	0.0	0.0

Note: OECD, Organisation for Economic Co-operation and Development.

Table F.3   Impact of full trade liberalization in industry: Rate of change of world indicators for 2015 (percent)

Indicator	Total
World agricultural trade	−6.2
World trade	1.0
World welfare	0.0

Table F.4   Impact of full trade liberalization in industry: Rate of change of macroeconomic indicators for 2015 (percent)

Country/zone	Allocation efficiency gains	Terms-of-trade gains	Welfare
Australia/New Zealand	0.1	0.4	0.3
Canada	0.4	0.1	−0.3
Developed Asia	0.4	0.2	0.2
EU 25	0.1	0.0	−0.3
United States	0.0	0.0	0.1
Rest of OECD	0.0	0.3	0.2
Argentina	0.1	−0.4	−1.1
Brazil	0.1	−0.3	−0.3
China	0.1	0.1	−0.2
Developing Asia	0.3	−0.4	0.2
India	0.8	−0.7	0.1
Mexico	1.0	−0.3	−0.5
Rest of Latin America	0.7	−0.4	0.0
Rest of Middle East and North Africa	0.7	−0.2	0.7
Rest of the World	0.6	0.0	−0.2
Southern African Customs Union	0.1	0.3	−0.7
Tunisia	0.3	−0.3	0.5
Bangladesh	1.6	−0.9	1.3
Rest of Sub-Saharan Africa	0.6	−0.4	−0.1
Zambia	1.5	−2.4	0.5

Note: OECD, Organisation for Economic Co-operation and Development.

Appendix G

Decomposition of Full Trade Liberalization, by Instrument

Table G.1   Impact of full elimination of import tariffs: Rate of change of world indicators for 2015 (percent)

Indicator	Total
World agricultural trade	39.5
World trade	9.0
World welfare	0.23

Table G.2   Impact of full elimination of import tariffs: Rate of change of macroeconomic indicators for 2015 (percent)

Country/zone	Allocation efficiency gains	Terms-of-trade gains	Welfare
Australia/New Zealand	0.0	1.0	0.5
Canada	0.4	−0.1	0.1
Developed Asia	2.0	0.1	1.5
EU 25	0.2	0.0	0.0
United States	0.0	0.0	0.0
Rest of OECD	1.0	0.2	1.0
Argentina	0.1	0.0	−0.2
Brazil	0.0	0.2	−0.4
China	0.2	0.5	−0.2
Developing Asia	0.7	0.0	0.5
India	1.5	−0.9	0.3
Mexico	0.6	−0.4	0.0
Rest of Latin America	0.7	−0.3	−0.1
Rest of Middle East and North Africa	0.8	−0.4	0.2
Rest of the World	0.7	−0.2	0.2
Southern African Customs Union	0.3	0.5	0.5
Tunisia	0.0	−0.4	−0.4
Bangladesh	1.0	−1.4	0.4
Rest of Sub-Saharan Africa	1.1	−1.0	−0.5
Zambia	0.8	−1.0	−0.5

Note: OECD, Organisation for Economic Co-operation and Development.

Table G.3   Impact of a full elimination of domestic support: Rate of change of world indicators for 2015 (percent)

Indicator	Total
World agricultural trade	−8.2
World trade	−6.1
World welfare	−0.04

Table G.4   Impact of full elimination of domestic support: Rate of change of macroeconomic indicators for 2015 (percent)

Country/zone	Allocation efficiency gains	Terms-of-trade gains	Welfare
Australia/New Zealand	0.1	0.3	0.1
Canada	0.3	0.2	−0.3
Developed Asia	0.4	−0.1	−0.1
EU 25	0.0	−0.1	−0.3
Rest of OECD	0.0	−0.1	0.0
United States	0.0	0.0	0.0
Argentina	0.1	−0.2	−0.7
Brazil	0.0	−0.1	0.3
China	−0.3	0.6	0.2
Developing Asia	0.1	−0.1	0.0
India	0.0	0.0	0.5
Mexico	0.7	−0.1	−0.4
Rest of Latin America	0.0	0.1	0.2
Rest of Middle East and North Africa	0.3	0.0	0.7
Rest of the World	0.2	0.1	0.2
Southern African Customs Union	−0.1	0.0	−0.8
Tunisia	0.5	0.2	1.3
Bangladesh	0.5	0.4	1.4
Rest of Sub-Saharan Africa	0.1	0.3	0.9
Zambia	1.0	−1.1	1.4

Note: OECD, Organisation for Economic Co-operation and Development.

Table G.5   Impact of full elimination of export subsidies: Rate of change of world indicators for 2015 (percent)

Indicator	Total
World agricultural trade	−5.6
World trade	−1.0
World welfare	−0.1

Table G.6.   Impact of full elimination of export subsidies: Rate of change of macroeconomic indicators for 2015 (percent)

Country/zone	Allocation efficiency gains	Terms-of-trade gains	Welfare
Australia/New Zealand	0.0	−0.1	−0.1
Canada	−0.1	−0.1	−0.2
Developed Asia	−0.1	−0.1	−0.2
EU 25	0.0	0.0	0.0
United States	0.0	−0.1	−0.1
Rest of OECD	−0.1	−0.1	−0.3
Argentina	−0.1	−0.4	−0.7
Brazil	0.0	−0.2	−0.2
China	−1.0	1.0	−0.8
Developing Asia	−0.1	0.1	−0.1
India	−0.1	0.1	0.1
Mexico	−0.1	0.1	−0.2
Rest of Latin America	0.0	0.0	0.0
Rest of Middle East and North Africa	0.0	−0.2	−0.1
Rest of the World	0.3	−0.2	−0.3
Southern African Customs Union	0.0	0.0	−0.1
Tunisia	0.2	0.3	0.6
Bangladesh	0.0	0.3	0.6
Rest of Sub-Saharan Africa	−0.1	−0.2	−0.4
Zambia	0.0	0.0	0.0

Note: OECD, Organisation for Economic Co-operation and Development.

Methodology for Assessing the Impact of Full Trade Liberalization by CGEM

This appendix provides synoptic tables on recent assessments (since 2001) of the impact of full trade liberalization and of the DDA on world welfare and poverty.[1]

A study might contain several modeling exercises corresponding to different theoretical structures. The assessment by Diao, Somwaru, and Roe (2001) is carried out using a static and a dynamic version. The two *Global Economic Prospects* from the World Bank (2002, 2004a) both utilize a dynamic framework; but the second exercise supposes a positive relation between trade openness and factor productivity. Cline (2004) exercise 1 corresponds to a static model with constant return to scale, whereas Cline (2004) 2 assesses expected benefits from trade liberalization using a steady state dynamic model in which capital increases until the rate of return on investment returns to the preliberalization level.

Tables H.1 and H.2 present three experiments of the Doha Agenda by Anderson, Martin, and Van der Mensbrugghe (2005a): the first one concerns liberalization only in agriculture, the second one adds a sensitive products clause, and the third adds to the first experiment liberalization in industry. Bouët, Mevel, and Orden (2005) present two alternative scenarios, the ambitious scenario and the unambitious one, to evaluate the potential area of negotiation in the last U.S. and EU proposals.

The columns in these tables indicate technical features of the experiment conducted (either full liberalization or the implementation of a potential DDA), the

---

[1]In the case of World Bank (2004a), it is a pro-poor scenario, which would imply elimination of export subsidies, decoupling all domestic support, and a significant cut in tariffs: rich countries would be subject to a maximum tariff of 10 percent in agriculture (5 percent in industry), with an average target of 5 percent (1 percent). For developing countries, the caps would be 15 percent (10 percent), with an average of 10 percent (5 percent).

CGEM under which the experiment was carried out, the geographic and sectoral decompositions (the first value is the number of trading zones, the second is the number of sectors), and the data utilized. All simulations are based on the GTAP database, either the GTAP 5 version accounting for 1997, or the GTAP 6 version, for 2001. This database may be improved (in this case, the notation "+ . . ." is added). For example, Bouët et al. (2005) utilize the GTAP 5 database but replace GTAP tariffs by MacMap-HS6 data and construct an original dataset of domestic support for the EU and the United States. Moreover, they simulate a pre-experiment shock for 2005, which includes not only these previous changes, but also the EBA initiative and AGOA, the end of the Uruguay Round, the phasing out of the Multi-Fibre Arrangement and the enlargement of the EU. If these liberalization shocks are not included before the experiment is conducted, the impact on trade and thus the benefits of openness would be overstated.

The amount of world benefits that can be expected from trade liberalization is not the only worthwhile information to be studied. Other points are of key importance: Is agriculture the main source of benefits? Must negotiators concentrate their efforts on market access, domestic support, or export subsidies? What kind of countries will be the main beneficiaries? Are expected benefits coming from liberalizing developed countries' trade policy or that of developing countries? Tables H.1 and H.2 give different macroeconomic results. The seventh and eighth rows of Table H.1 focus on world welfare that results from this experiment. The increase in this indicator is assessed in U.S. dollars, then in percentage. To address the previous questions, rows five to eight decompose this increase in world welfare into parts coming from liberalizing agriculture, coming from improving market access, benefiting developing countries, and coming from liberalization in developing countries.

Presenting the contribution of each distortion in potential welfare increase is not strictly consistent: if referring to the theory of second best, the elimination of one distortion in a world where several conditions for a Pareto optimum are not fulfilled does not necessarily entail a welfare improvement. On the contrary, adding a distortion may increase welfare. As a result, simultaneously eliminating tariffs, domestic support, and export subsidies does not imply the same increase in welfare as the sum of the three separate changes in economic policy. Nevertheless, studies on the expected benefits of trade liberalization frequently present this sort of additive decomposition. I retain this presentation in my review of the literature but adopt a more consistent way of presenting results in the central experiment.[2]

In Tables H.1 and H.2, the following three rows concern other macroeconomic information: increase in world trade, increase in world agricultural trade,

---

[2]The decomposition technique that is used in all these studies has been inspired by Harrison, Horridge, and Pearson (2000).

and variation of world agricultural prices. This last information is crucial, because a frequent criticism of trade liberalization is that it will entail an augmentation of these prices such that net food-importing countries could see a reduction in their welfare. The subsequent row in the tables indicates whether there are losers in this process in terms of national welfare.

Finally, the last row indicates the impact on world poverty (using the US$2.00 per day definition) when available. This result is obviously a key issue of this debate.

Table H.1   Results of recent assessments of the impact of full trade liberalization

	Dessus, Fukasaku, and Safadi (1999)	Dessus, Fukasaku, and Safadi (1999)	Dee and Hanslow (2000)	Anderson et al. (2000)	Diao, Somwaru, and Roe (2001) scenario 1	Diao, Somwaru, and Roe (2001) scenario 2	World Bank (2002) scenario 1	World Bank (2002) scenario 2
Experiment[a]	Full tariff	Full tariff	Full	Full	Full	Full	Full	Full
Model used	Linkage	Linkage	FTAP	GTAP	Agricultural USDA-ERS model	Agricultural USDA-ERS model	Linkage	Linkage
Static/dynamic	Dynamic	Dynamic	Dynamic	Dynamic	Static	Dynamic	Dynamic	Dynamic
Specific feature		TO/TFP	FDI					TO/TFP
Geographic × sector decomposition	16 × 4	16 × 4	19 × 3		12 × 9	12 × 9	15 × 20	15 × 20
Year of data	1995	1995	1995+	1995	1997+	1997+	1997	1997
World welfare (US$ billion)	82	1212	134	254	31	56	355	852
Total (percent)	0.20	3.10	0.32	0.62	0.13	0.24	0.90	2.10
Agriculture (percent)	n.a.	n.a.	n.a.	65	n.a.	n.a.	69	71
Tariffs (percent)	n.a.	n.a.	n.a.	n.a.	n.a.	n.a.		
Beneficial to developing countries (percent)	22	38	n.a.	43	8	38	52	65
Stemming from trade liberalization in developing countries (percent)	n.a.	n.a.	n.a.	45	n.a.	n.a.	55	66
World trade (percent)	n.a.	n.a.	n.a.	n.a.	n.a.	n.a.	—	17
World agricultural trade (percent)	n.a.	n.a.	n.a.	n.a.	n.a.	15		
World agricultural prices (percent)	n.a.	n.a.	n.a.	n.a.	n.a.	12		
Potential losers	n.a.	None	n.a.	n.a.	Mexico, Rest of the World	None	None	None
Change in poverty headcount (million)	n.a.	n.a.	n.a.	n.a.	n.a.	n.a.	−320	n.a.

Notes: FDI, foreign direct investment; FTAP, Foreign Direct Investment Trade Analysis Project; GTAP, Global Trade Analysis Project; HRT, Harrison-Rutherford-Tarr; n.a., not applicable; SS, steady state; TO/TFP, trade openess/total factor productivity; USDA-ERS, U.S. Department of Agriculture–Economic Research Service.
[a]Entries refer to extent or type of liberalization for each model.

	World Bank (2004a) scenario 1	World Bank (2004a) scenario 2	Cline (2004) scenario 1	Cline (2004) scenario 2	Beghin and Van der Mensbrugghe (2003)	Anderson, Martin, and Van der Mensbrugghe (2005a)	Francois, Von Meijl, and Van Tongeren (2005)	Hertel and Keeney (2005)	Bouët, Mevel and Orden (2005)	Bouët (2006)
	Pro-poor Linkage	Pro-poor Linkage	Full HRT	Full HRT	Full Linkage	Full Linkage	Full GTAP 5	Full GTAP-Agr	Full MIRAGE	Full MIRAGE
	Dynamic	Dynamic	Static	Dynamic	Dynamic	Dynamic	Dynamic	Static	Dynamic	Dynamic
		TO/TFP		SS						
	23 × 1997+	23 × 1997+	25 × 22 1997	25 × 22 1997	23 × 22 1997+	27 × 25 2001+	16 × 17 1997+	30 × 2001+	41 × 18 2001+	20 × 17 2001+
	291	518	228	614	385	287	163	84	157	99.6
	0.80	1.40	0.93	2.50	0.90	0.70	0.43	n.a.	0.50	0.33
	66	69	57	n.a.	69	63	65	66	n.a.	n.a.
			n.a.	n.a.	99	93	91	95	n.a.	n.a.
	55	67	38	47	56	30	8	26	n.a.	n.a.
	62	62	44	n.a.	n.a.	45	58	n.a.	n.a.	n.a.
	10				—	n.a.	12	7.50	12.10	5.25
	32				74	76		21	n.a.	34
					—	n.a.		n.a.	n.a.	2.5/11
	None	None	Malaysia, Mexico	Malaysia, China	None	None	South America, China, India	Philippines, Bangladesh, Rest of Latin America, Mozambique, Rest of Sub-Saharan Africa	China, Venezuela, Bangladesh, Madagascar, Mozambique, Zambia	Canada, EU, Argentina, Mexico, Southern African Customs Union
	−144	n.a.	−110	−440		−72	n.a.	n.a.	n.a.	n.a.

Table H.2 Assessing the impact of a DDA by CGEM

	Bouët et al. (2005)	Fontagné, Guérin, and Jean (2005)	Bchir, Fontagné, and Jean (2005)	Francois, Van Meijl, and Van Tongeren (2005)	Anderson, Martin, and Van der Mensbrugghe (2005a) scenario 1	Anderson, Martin, and Van der Mensbrugghe (2005a) scenario 2	Anderson, Martin, and Van der Mensbrugghe (2005a) scenario 3	Bouët, Mevel, and Orden (2005) scenario 1	Bouët, Mevel, and Orden (2005) scenario 2
Experiment	DDA agriculture	DDA	DDA industry	DDA	DDA agriculture	DDA agriculture + SSP	DDA	DDA	DDA
Model used	MIRAGE	MIRAGE	MIRAGE	GTAP 5	Linkage	Linkage	Linkage	MIRAGE	MIRAGE
Static/dynamic	Static	Dynamic	Static	Dynamic	Dynamic	Dynamic	Dynamic	Dynamic	Dynamic
Geographic × sector decomposition	11 × 30	7 × 57	22 × 20	16 × 17	27 × 25	27 × 25	27 × 25	41 × 18	41 × 18
Year of data	1997+	1997+	2001+	1997+	2001+	2001+	2001+	2001+	2001+
World welfare (US$ billion)	23	146	12	100	75	18	96	41	104
Total (percent)	0.08	0.51	0.04	0.34	0.18	0.04	0.23	0.17	0.33
Agriculture (percent)	n.a.	n.a.	n.a.	66	—	—	—	n.a.	n.a.
Tariffs (percent)	n.a.	n.a.	n.a.	91	n.a.	n.a.	99.70	n.a.	n.a.
Beneficial to developing countries (percent)	21	n.a.	14	11	12				
Stemming from liberalization in developing countries (percent)						loss	17		
World trade		n.a.	n.a.	67	n.a.	n.a.	n.a.	n.a.	n.a.
World agricultural trade	6.10	n.a.	3.20	n.a.	n.a.	n.a.	n.a.	2.0	4.1
World agricultural prices	0.3/26.0	n.a.	n.a.	n.a.	n.a.	n.a.	n.a.	n.a.	n.a.
Potential losers	Mediterranean countries, Sub-Saharan Africa	None	Canada, Brazil, China, India, Mexico, Rest of Latin America	South America, China	Hong Kong, Singapore, Bangladesh, China, Vietnam, Russia, Mexico	Hong Kong, Singapore, Bangladesh, China, Vietnam, Mexico, Russia, Rest of Sub-Saharan Africa, Middle East and North Africa	Hong Kong, Singapore, Bangladesh, China, Vietnam, Mexico, Russia, Rest of Sub-Saharan Africa	Venezuela, Zambia, Madagascar, Mozambique	Venezuela, Zambia
Change in poverty headcount (million)	n.a.	n.a.	n.a.	n.a.	−1.3	+0.3	−6.2	n.a.	n.a.

Notes: See Appendix H text for an explanation of this table. CGEM, computed general equilibrium model; DDA, Doha Development Agenda; GTAP, Global Trade Analysis Project; MIRAGE, Modeling International Relations under Applied General Equilibrium; n.a., not applicable; SSP, Sensitive and Special Products.

Custom Taxes as a Proportion of Gross Domestic Product

Table I.1   Custom taxes as a proportion of gross domestic product, by country (percent)

Country	Custom taxes/ gross domestic product	Country	Custom taxes/ gross domestic product
Singapore	0.0	Belgium	0.4
Luxembourg	0.1	Australia	0.5
France	0.1	Rest of Southeast Asia	0.5
Denmark	0.1	Argentina	0.5
Sweden	0.1	Poland	0.5
Finland	0.1	Indonesia	0.6
Greece	0.1	Latvia	0.6
Austria	0.1	Mexico	0.7
United States	0.1	Croatia	0.7
Germany	0.1	South Africa	0.7
Italy	0.1	Taiwan	0.7
Spain	0.1	Brazil	0.7
United Kingdom	0.2	Rest of Southern African	
Japan	0.2	Customs Union	0.7
Lithuania	0.2	Uganda	0.7
Canada	0.2	Uruguay	0.8
Ireland	0.2	Switzerland	0.8
Portugal	0.2	Hungary	0.8
Rest of Former Soviet Union	0.2	Slovakia	0.8
Netherlands	0.3	Chile	0.9
Bulgaria	0.3	Czech Republic	0.9
New Zealand	0.3	Philippines	0.9
Rest of European Free Trade Area	0.3	Colombia	0.9
Estonia	0.3	Russian Federation	0.9
Turkey	0.4	Peru	0.9
Botswana	0.4	Venezuela	1.0
Madagascar	0.4		*(continued)*

Country	Custom taxes/ gross domestic product	Country	Custom taxes/ gross domestic product
China	1.1	Rest of North Africa	2.0
Romania	1.1	Malawi	2.0
Rest of Middle East	1.1	Central America	2.1
Zimbabwe	1.2	Cyprus	2.1
Rest of Andean Pact	1.3	Thailand	2.3
Zambia	1.3	Slovenia	2.3
Korea	1.5	Albania	2.5
Tanzania	1.5	Rest of Europe	2.5
India	1.6	Rest of Sub-Saharan Africa	2.7
Sri Lanka	1.6	Malta	2.9
Rest of Free Trade Area of the Americas	1.6	Rest of Oceania	3.1
Malaysia	1.6	Morocco	3.2
Rest of South Asia	1.6	Vietnam	4.0
Rest of Latin America	1.6	Rest of Southern African Development Community	4.0
Rest of the Caribbean	1.7	Tunisia	4.3
Mozambique	1.7	Rest of North America	13.9
Bangladesh	1.9		

Source: GTAP 6 database (see Dimaranan 2006).

Model Option: No Pre-Experiment

Table J.1   Impact of a full trade liberalization from 2001: Rate of change of world indicators for 2015 (percent)

Indicator	Total
World agricultural imports	39.05
World trade	4.59
World welfare	0.45

Table J.2   Impact of full trade liberalization from 2001: Rate of change of macroeconomic indicators for 2015 (percent)

Country/zone	Allocation efficiency gains	Terms-of-trade gains	Welfare
Australia/New Zealand	0.1	1.5	1.1
Canada	0.7	0.3	0.1
Developed Asia	2.3	0.2	1.6
EU 25	0.2	0.0	0.0
United States	0.0	0.1	0.3
Rest of OECD	1.0	0.2	1.0
Argentina	0.4	0.7	0.5
Brazil	0.1	0.6	0.4
China	1.6	−1.0	0.9
Developing Asia	0.8	−0.1	0.6
India	1.6	−1.1	0.5
Mexico	1.4	−0.6	−0.2
Rest of Latin America	0.8	−0.2	0.0
Rest of Middle East and North Africa	1.3	−0.5	0.9
Rest of the World	1.0	0.0	0.0
Southern African Customs Union	0.3	0.6	−0.1
Tunisia	0.2	−1.0	−0.8
Bangladesh	1.8	−1.3	1.0
Rest of Sub-Saharan Africa	1.3	−0.5	0.7
Zambia	1.6	−2.5	0.1

Note: OECD, Organisation for Economic Co-operation and Development.

Table J.3   Impact of full trade liberalization from 2001: Rate of change of factor remuneration for 2015 (percent)

	Agriculture: Unskilled real wages	Industry: Unskilled real wages	Real return to capital	Real return to land	Real return to natural resources	Skilled real wages
Australia/New Zealand	10.9	2.2	−0.6	4.0	−4.8	1.4
Canada	−0.1	−0.2	−0.2	−24.3	4.2	0.1
Developed Asia	−2.7	2.1	1.6	−31.4	−6.4	2.5
EU 25	0.4	0.3	−0.6	−41.4	−3.4	0.1
United States	1.4	0.1	−0.2	−15.7	2.2	0.1
Rest of OECD	−4.6	0.9	0.9	−50.0	5.4	1.3
Argentina	10.5	2.6	−1.1	10.5	−10.7	−0.8
Brazil	9.5	1.7	−0.5	10.9	−9.5	0.2
China	−0.6	4.2	−2.2	−9.3	−21.3	6.6
Developing Asia	0.6	1.3	0.1	−6.0	−17.1	1.0
India	−1.7	1.8	−0.1	−4.8	−25.6	4.2
Mexico	−4.7	0.2	0.5	−23.6	−22.9	−1.8
Rest of Latin America	4.3	1.2	−1.3	7.9	−13.1	−0.1
Rest of Middle East and North Africa	−2.4	0.9	1.1	−7.5	−10.1	1.2
Rest of the World	−1.1	2.0	−2.5	−5.6	13.2	−0.3
Southern African Customs Union	5.0	0.9	−1.6	12.9	9.0	−0.2
Tunisia	0.2	−0.2	−0.4	−0.9	−5.5	−1.0
Bangladesh	1.0	0.6	0.7	1.8	−6.2	−0.3
Rest of Sub-Saharan Africa	0.7	1.8	−1.0	0.2	−4.4	1.5
Zambia	−4.2	−1.1	1.6	−8.9	−22.7	0.3

Note: OECD, Organisation for Economic Co-operation and Development.

Model Option: No Preferential Duties

Table K.1   Impact of full trade liberalization: Rate of change of world indicators for 2015 (percent)

Indicator	Total
World agricultural trade	30.61
World trade	4.11
World welfare	0.41

Table K.2   Impact of full trade liberalization from 2001: Rate of change of macroeconomic indicators for 2015 (percent)

Country/zone	Allocation efficiency gains	Terms-of-trade gains	Welfare
Argentina	0.3	0.3	−0.2
Australia/New Zealand	0.1	1.4	1.1
Canada	0.6	0.3	0.0
Developed Asia	1.8	0.0	1.1
EU 25	0.3	−0.1	−0.1
United States	0.0	0.2	0.2
Brazil	0.0	0.7	0.9
China	0.8	0.0	0.4
Developing Asia	1.2	−0.5	1.0
India	3.1	−1.5	1.3
Mexico	1.1	−0.1	−0.2
Rest of Latin America	3.0	−0.9	2.5
Rest of Middle East and North Africa	1.2	−0.6	0.6
Rest of OECD	1.1	−0.2	0.5
Rest of the World	1.0	−0.1	−0.3
Rest of Sub-Saharan Africa	1.1	0.5	2.0
Southern African Customs Union	0.4	1.9	2.7
Tunisia	6.6	−1.8	5.2
Bangladesh	1.7	−0.8	1.8
Zambia	1.7	−1.1	2.7

Note: OECD, Organisation for Economic Co-operation and Development.

Table K.3 Impact of full trade liberalization from 2001: Rate of change of factor remuneration for 2015 (percent)

Country/zone	Agriculture: Unskilled real wages	Industry: Unskilled real wages	Real return to capital	Real return to land	Real return to natural resources	Skilled real wages
Argentina	6.2	1.4	−1.4	2.9	−8.7	−1.6
Australia/New Zealand	11.5	2.3	−0.6	3.8	−12.4	1.5
Canada	0.2	−0.1	−0.4	−24.3	3.8	0.0
Developed Asia	−2.6	1.6	1.1	−30.1	−0.9	1.8
EU 25	−0.6	0.5	−0.8	−42.4	−3.6	−0.2
Rest of OECD	−6.7	0.9	0.2	−50.9	−1.9	1.3
USA	1.1	0.2	−0.2	−17.1	1.8	0.1
Brazil	6.1	1.9	1.0	1.4	−9.7	1.1
China	−1.6	1.1	−0.6	−7.5	−25.5	3.1
Developing Asia	−0.5	0.2	0.1	−7.1	−19.7	0.9
India	−0.4	3.3	−0.5	−4.4	−29.9	6.5
Mexico	−4.0	0.6	0.8	−23	−13.2	−2.0
Rest of Latin America	6.0	4.5	0.0	4.9	−19.8	3.9
Rest of Middle East and North Africa	−1.5	1.3	0.1	−6.7	−11.3	1.1
Rest of the World	−1.8	1.3	−3.1	−6.9	22.4	−1.6
Rest of Sub-Saharan Africa	3.0	3.2	0.7	2.4	−2.6	2.8
Southern African Customs Union	6.2	3.2	2.1	10.3	−4.3	2.8
Tunisia	−1.1	5.5	7.6	−14.7	−25	7.9
Bangladesh	2.4	1.9	0.3	3.1	−3.1	1.2
Zambia	−0.9	1.0	4.0	−6.3	−26.9	3.7

Note: OECD, Organisation for Economic Co-operation and Development.

Model Option: Higher Trade Elasticities

Table L.1   Impact of full trade liberalization: Rate of change of world indicators for 2015 (percent)

Indicator	Total
World agricultural trade	57.07
World trade	5.25
World welfare	0.44

Table L.2   Impact of full trade liberalization from 2001: Rate of change of macroeconomic indicators for 2015 (percent)

Country/zone	Allocation efficiency gains	Terms-of-trade gains	Welfare
Australia/New Zealand	0.1	1.4	0.9
Canada	0.7	0.1	0.0
Developed Asia	2.3	0.1	1.8
EU 25	0.3	−0.1	−0.1
United States	0.0	0.1	0.2
Rest of OECD	1.3	−0.1	1.1
Argentina	0.3	0.4	0.0
Brazil	0.1	0.7	0.5
China	0.8	0.1	0.6
Developing Asia	1.1	−0.1	0.6
India	2.4	−1.1	1.0
Mexico	1.5	−0.6	−0.2
Rest of Latin America	0.5	0.1	0.1
Rest of Middle East and North Africa	1.5	−0.3	1.4
Rest of the World	1.2	−0.2	0.6
Southern African Customs Union	0.4	0.6	0.0
Tunisia	0.4	−0.5	0.3
Bangladesh	2.0	−1.1	1.7
Rest of Sub-Saharan Africa	1.9	−0.8	1.2
Zambia	1.8	−2.1	0.7

Note: OECD, Organisation for Economic Co-operation and Development.

Table L.3   Impact of full trade liberalization from 2001: Rate of change of factor remuneration for 2015 (percent)

Country/zone	Agriculture: Unskilled real wages	Industry: Unskilled real wages	Real return to capital	Real return to land	Real return to natural resources	Skilled real wages
Australia/New Zealand	10.6	2.1	−0.8	4.8	−3.9	1.2
Canada	−0.7	−0.2	−0.3	−23.0	2.0	−0.1
Developed Asia	−2.1	2.4	1.7	−35.1	−4.9	2.9
EU 25	−0.4	0.4	−0.7	−43.0	−3.9	0.0
United States	0.6	0.1	−0.2	−17.0	1.9	0.1
Rest of OECD	−4.7	1.2	0.8	−51.8	0.6	1.6
Argentina	6.6	1.7	−1.5	4.8	−5.7	−1.4
Brazil	9.5	2.1	−0.7	6.6	−9.1	0.6
China	−0.9	2.5	−1.8	−7.9	−16.1	4.3
Developing Asia	−0.3	1.5	0.3	−9.3	−14.3	1.5
India	−3.4	2.6	1.6	−7.8	−17.3	5.4
Mexico	−5.7	0.4	0.6	−26.0	−21.2	−1.7
Rest of Latin America	5.9	1.7	−1.5	11.8	−11.9	−0.2
Rest of Middle East and North Africa	−3.4	1.5	1.6	−9.5	−8.2	2.1
Rest of the World	−0.4	2.3	−1.6	−3.2	8.5	0.7
Southern African Customs Union	5.6	1.1	−1.7	17.1	6.2	−0.1
Tunisia	0.4	1.0	0.7	−1.8	−7.4	0.4
Bangladesh	0.3	1.7	1.7	−0.1	−2.5	1.0
Rest of Sub-Saharan Africa	0.1	2.3	−0.4	0.5	−2.9	2.0
Zambia	−6.3	−0.4	2.8	−11.8	−14.1	1.1

Note: OECD, Organisation for Economic Co-operation and Development.

Model Option: Trade Increases
Factor Productivity

Table M.1   Impact of full trade liberalization: Rate of change of world indicators for 2015 (percent)

Indicator	Total
World agricultural imports	32.49
World merchandise trade	4.87
World welfare	0.59

Table M.2.   Impact of full trade liberalization: Rate of change of macroeconomic indicators for 2015 (percent)

Country/zone	Allocation efficiency gains	Terms-of-trade gains	Welfare
Australia/New Zealand	0.0	1.3	0.3
Canada	0.7	0.2	0.3
Developed Asia	2.2	0.1	1.3
EU 25	0.2	−0.1	0.2
Rest of OECD	1.0	0.1	1.2
United States	0.0	0.1	0.3
Argentina	0.2	0.3	−0.4
Brazil	0.0	0.4	−0.2
China	0.9	0.3	1.9
Developing Asia	0.8	−0.2	0.5
India	1.7	−1.0	3.2
Mexico	1.3	−0.5	0.4
Rest of Latin America	0.8	−0.2	0.6
Rest of Middle East and North Africa	1.2	−0.4	1.5
Rest of the World	0.9	−0.1	0.9
Southern African Customs Union	0.3	0.5	0.0
Tunisia	0.3	−0.3	0.0
Bangladesh	1.8	−1.0	2.5
Rest of Sub-Saharan Africa	1.4	−0.7	1.7
Zambia	1.6	−2.3	−0.6

Note: OECD, Organisation for Economic Co-operation and Development.

Table M.3 Impact of full trade liberalization: Rate of change of factor remuneration for 2015 (percent)

Country/zone	Agriculture: Unskilled real wages	Industry: Unskilled real wages	Real return to capital	Real return to land	Real return to natural resources	Skilled real wages
Australia/New Zealand	8.6	1.5	−1.3	2.1	−4.2	0.8
Canada	−0.4	0.1	0.0	−25.1	4.3	0.2
Developed Asia	−3.1	2.0	1.3	−30.8	−4.1	2.3
EU 25	0.0	0.6	−0.4	−41.8	−3.0	0.1
Rest of OECD	−4.2	1.1	1.1	−48.8	5.4	1.4
United States	0.5	0.2	−0.2	−17.6	2.3	0.2
Argentina	5.0	1.4	−1.9	1.8	−6.9	−0.9
Brazil	6.3	1.5	−1.3	3.8	−8.7	0.5
China	0.0	3.5	−0.4	−7.2	−18.0	6.4
Developing Asia	0.4	1.3	−0.1	−6.1	−16.6	1.3
India	−0.1	4.4	3.0	−4.6	−17.9	7.9
Mexico	−3.9	1.1	1.0	−23.4	−23.2	−0.3
Rest of Latin America	4.3	2.0	−0.5	6.8	−13.2	0.9
Rest of Middle East and North Africa	−1.8	1.8	1.8	−7.0	−11.6	2.3
Rest of the World	−1.2	2.4	−1.1	−6.1	11.6	1.3
Southern African Customs Union	4.4	1.1	−1.5	11.1	9.0	0.2
Tunisia	0.4	0.6	0.3	−1.6	−6.9	0.0
Bangladesh	1.9	2.8	2.5	0.4	−6.5	2.6
Rest of Sub-Saharan Africa	1.0	2.6	0.5	0.0	−4.5	2.9
Zambia	−5.3	−1.6	0.9	−10.4	−23.8	0.3

Note: OECD, Organisation for Economic Co-operation and Development.

References

Ackerman, F. 2005. The shrinking gains from trade: A critical assessment of Doha Round projections. Global Development and Environment Institute Working Paper 05-01, Tufts University, Medford, Mass., U.S.A.

Anderson, J. E. 1979. A theoretical foundation for the gravity equation. *American Economic Review* 69 (1): 106–116.

Anderson, J. E., and E. van Wincoop. 2003. Gravity with gravitas: A solution to the Border Puzzle. *American Economic Review* 93 (1): 170–192.

Anderson, K., W. Martin, and D. Van der Mensbrugghe. 2005a. Market and welfare implications of Doha reform scenarios. In *Trade reform and the Doha Agenda,* ed. K. Anderson and W. Martin. Washington, D.C.: World Bank.

———. 2005b. Doha merchandise trade reform: What's at stake for developing countries? Plenary paper for the Eighth Annual Conference on Global Economic Analysis (GTAP), Lübeck, June 9–11.

———. 2005c. Global impacts of the Doha scenarios on poverty. In *Putting development back into the Doha Agenda: Poverty impacts of a WTO agreement,* ed. T. W. Hertel and L. A. Winters. Washington, D.C.: World Bank.

Anderson, K., J. Francois, T. W. Hertel, B. Hoekman, and W. Martin. 2000. Potential gains from trade reform in the new millennium. Paper for the Third Annual Conference on Global Economic Analysis (GTAP), Monash University, Melbourne, June 27–20.

Armington, P. 1969. A theory of demand for products distinguished by place of origin. *IMF Staff Papers* 16: 159–178.

Bawden, D. L. 1966. A spatial equilibrium model of international trade. *Journal of Farm Economics* 48: 862–874.

Bchir, M. H., L. Fontagné, and S. Jean. 2005. *From bound duties to actual protection: Industrial protection in the Doha Round.* CEPII Working Paper 2005-12. Paris: Centre d'Etudes Prospectives et d'Informations Internationales.

Bchir, M. H., Y. Decreux, J.-L. Guérin, and S. Jean. 2002. *MIRAGE, a general equilibrium model for trade policy analysis.* CEPII Working Paper 2002-17. Paris: Centre d'Etudes Prospectives et d'Informations Internationales.

Beghin, J. C., and D. Van der Mensbrugghe. 2003. Global agricultural reform: What is at stake? In *Global agricultural trade and developing countries,* ed. M. A. Aksoy and J. C. Beghin. Washington, D.C.: World Bank.

Bergstrand, J. H. 1989. The general equation, monopolistic competition and the factor-proportions theory in international trade. *Review of Economics and Statistics* 71: 1, 143–153.

———. 1990. The Heckscher-Ohlin-Samuelson model, the Linder hypothesis and the determinants of bilateral intra-industry trade. *Economic Journal* 100: 1216–1229.

Bouët, A. 2001. Research and development, voluntary export restriction and tariffs. *European Economic Review* 45: 323–336.

———. 2006. What can the poor expect from trade liberalization? Opening the "black box" of trade modeling. MTID Discussion Paper 93. Washington, D.C.: International Food Policy Research Institute.

Bouët, A., S. Mevel, and D. Orden. 2005. More or less ambition? Modeling the development impact of US-EU agricultural proposals in the Doha Round. IFPRI Information Brief. Washington, D.C.: International Food Policy Research Institute.

Bouët, A., J.-C. Bureau, Y. Decreux, and S. Jean. 2005. Multilateral agricultural trade liberalization: The contrasting fortunes of developing countries in the Doha Round. *World Economy* 28–29: 1329–1354.

Bouët, A., Y. Decreux, L. Fontagné, S. Jean, and D. Laborde. 2006. Tariff duties in GTAP 6: The MacMap-HS6 database, sources and methodology. In *Global trade, assistance, and production: The GTAP 6 data base,* ed. B. V. Dimaranan. West Lafayette, Ind., U.S.A.: Center for Global Trade Analysis, Purdue University.

———. 2008. Assessing applied protection across the world. *Review of International Economics.* Forthcoming.

Bourguignon, F., V. Levin, and D. Rosenblatt. 2004. Declining international inequality and economic divergence: Reviewing the evidence through different lenses. *Economie internationale* 100: 13–26.

Brenton, P. 2003. The value of trade preferences: The economic impact of Everything but Arms. World Bank, Washington, D.C. Mimeo.

Brenton, P., and M. Manchin. 2003. Making EU trade agreements work: The role of rules of origin. *World Economy* 26: 755–769.

Brenton, P., and T. Ikezuki. 2004. The impact of agricultural trade preferences, with particular attention to the least-developed countries. In *Global agricultural trade and developing countries,* ed. M. A. Aksoy and J. C. Beghin. Washington, D.C.: World Bank.

Candau, F., and S. Jean. 2005. *What are EU trade preferences worth for Sub-Saharan Africa and other developing countries?* CEPII Working Paper 2005-19. Paris: Centre d'Etudes Prospectives et d'Informations Internationales.

Candau, F., L. Fontagné, and S. Jean. 2004. The utilisation rate of references in the EU. 7th Global Economic Analysis Conference, June 17–19, Washington, D.C.

Cline, W. R. 2004. *Trade policy and global poverty.* Washington, D.C.: Institute for International Economics.

Cockburn, J. C. 2001. *Trade liberalization and poverty in Nepal: A computable general equilibrium microsimulation analysis.* Cahier de Recherche 01-18. Quebec: Centre de Recherche Economie et Finance Appliqués, Université de Laval.

Cogneau, D., and A.-S. Robilliard. 2000. *Growth, distribution and poverty in Madagascar: Learning from a microsimulation model in a general equilibrium framework.* IFPRI Trade and Macroeconomics Division Discussion Paper 61. Washington, D.C.: International Food Policy Research Institute.

Cororaton, C., and J. C. Cockburn. 2004. *Trade reform and poverty in the Philippines: A computable general equilibrium microsimulation analysis.* Manila: Philippine Institute for Development Studies.

Deardorff, A. V. 1998. Determinants of bilateral trade: Does gravity equation work in a neoclassical world? In *The regionalization of the world economy,* ed. J. A. Frankel. Chicago: University of Chicago for the National Bureau of Economic Research.

Dee, P., and K. Hanslow. 2000. *Multilateral liberalisation of services trade.* Staff Research Paper. Melbourne: Australia Productivity Commission.

De Gorter, H., and I. Sheldon. 2000. Issues in reforming tariff-rate import quotas in the agreement on agriculture in the WTO. *Agricultural and Resource Economics Review* 29 (1): 54–57.

Dessus, S., K. Fukasaku, and R. Safadi. 1999. *La libéralisation multilaterale des droits de douane et les pays en developpement.* Cahier de Politique Economique 18. Paris: Centre de Developpement de l'OCDE.

Devadoss, S., A. H. Aguiar, S. R. Shook, and J. Araji. 2005. A spatial equilibrium analysis of US-Canadian disputes on the world softwood lumber market. *Canadian Journal of Agricultural Economics* 53 (2–3): 177–192.

Deverajan, S., and D. Van der Mensbrugghe. 2000. Trade reform in South Africa: Impact on households. Paper prepared for the Conference on Poverty and the International Economy, Stockholm, October 20–21.

Diao, X., A. Somwaru, and T. Roe. 2001. A global analysis of agricultural reform in WTO member countries. In special issue: *Agricultural policy reform—The road ahead. Agricultural Economic Report* 802: 25–42.

Diao, X., E. Diaz-Bonilla, S. Robinson, and D. Orden. 2005. Tell me where it hurts, an' I'll tell you who to call: Industrialized countries' agricultural policies and developing countries. IFPRI Discussion Paper 84. Washington, D.C.: International Food Policy Research Institute.

Dimaranan, B. V., ed. 2006. *Global trade assistance and production: The GTAP 6 data base.* West Lafayette, Ind., U.S.A.: Center for Global Trade Analysis.

Directorate General for Agricultural and Rural Development, European Commission. 2005. *AVE—Ad valorem equivalents.* Monitoring Agri-Trade Policy—Brief, April. Brussels: European Commission.

Fontagné, L., J.-L. Guérin, and S. Jean. 2005. Market access liberalization in the Doha Round: Scenarios and assessment *World Economy* 28 (8): 1073–1094.

Fontagné, L., M. Pajot, and J.-M. Pasteels. 2001. Potentiel de commerce entre économies hétérogènes: un petit mode d'emploi des modèles de gravité. Paris I, Panthéon-Sorbonne, Théorie et Applications en Microéconomie et Macroéconomie, Paris. Mimeo.

Francois, J. F., and K. H. Hall. 1993. COMPAS: Commercial Policy Analysis System. Washington, D.C.: U.S. International Trade Commission.

———. 1997. Partial equilibrium modeling. In *Applied methods for trade policy analysis: A handbook,* ed. J. F. Francois and K. A. Reinert. Cambridge: Cambridge University Press.

Francois, J., H. Van Meijl, and F. Van Tongeren. 2005. Trade liberalization in the Doha Development Round. *Economic Policy* 20 (42): 349–391.

Harrison, G. W., T. F. Rutherford, and D. G. Tarr. 1997. Quantifying the Uruguay Round. *Economic Journal* 107: 1405–1430.

————. 2001. Trade liberalization, poverty and efficient equity. *Journal of Development Economics* 71-1: 97–128.

Harrison, W. J., J. M. Horridge, and K. Pearson. 2000. Decomposing simulation results with respect to exogenous shocks. *Computational Economics* 15: 227–249.

Hertel, T. W. 2000. Potential gains from reducing trade barriers in manufacturing, services and agriculture. *Federal Reserve Bulletin, Federal Reserve Bank of St. Louis,* July–August, p. 77–100.

Hertel, T. W., and R. Keeney. 2005. What's at stake: The relative importance of import barriers, export subsidies and domestic support. In *Putting development back into the Doha Agenda: Poverty impacts of a WTO agreement,* ed. T. W. Hertel and L. A. Winters. Washington, D.C.: World Bank.

Hertel, T. W., M. Ivanic, P. V. Preckel, and J. A. L. Cranfield. 2000. The earning effects of multilateral trade liberalization: Implications for poverty. *World Bank Economic Review* 18 (2): 205–236.

Hertel, T. W., D. Hummels, M. Ivanic, and R. Keeney. 2003. *How confident can we be in CGE-based assessments of free trade agreements?* GTAP Working Paper 26. West Lafayette, Ind., U.S.A.: Center for Global Trade Analysis, Purdue University.

Hufbauer, G., and K. A. Elliott. 1994. *Measuring the costs of protection in the United States.* Washington, D.C.: Institute for International Economics.

Jean, S., D. Laborde, and W. Martin. 2005. Consequences of alternative formulas for agricultural tariff cuts. In *Trade reform and the Doha Agenda,* ed. K. Anderson and W. Martin. Washington, D.C.: World Bank.

Kahn, F. C. 1997. Household disaggregation. In *Applied methods for trade policy analysis—A handbook,* ed. J. F. Francois and K. A. Reinert. Cambridge: Cambridge University Press.

Kuznets, S. 1955. Economic growth and income inequality. *American Economic Review* 45: 1–28.

Levin, J. 2000. Kenya—Poverty eradication through transfers. Paper prepared for the Conference on Poverty and the International Economy, October 20–21, Stockholm.

Martin, W., and D. Mitra. 2001. Productivity growth and convergence in agriculture and manufacturing. *Economic Development and Cultural Change* 49 (2): 403–422.

Matthews, A., and C. Laroche Dupraz. 2001. Agricultural tariff quotas as a development instrument. *Economie Internationale* 87: 89–106.

McCalla, A. F., and T. E. Josling. 1985. *Agricultural policies and world markets.* New York: MacMillan.

McCallum, J. 1995. National borders matter: Canada–US regional trade patterns. *American Economic Review* 85 (3): 615–623.

Messerlin, P. 2001. *Measuring the costs of protection in Europe: European commercial policy in the 2000s.* Washington, D.C.: Institute for International Economics.

Milanovic, B. 2005. *Worlds apart: Measuring international and global inequality.* Princeton, N.J.: Princeton University Press.

Oliveira-Martins, J. 1994. Market structure, trade, and industry wages. *OECD Economic Studies* 22: 132–154.

Oliveira-Martins, J., and S. Scarpetta. 1999. Mark-up ratios in manufacturing industries: Estimates for 14 OECD countries. OECD Economics Department Working Paper 162. Organisation for Economic Co-operation and Development, Paris.

Oliveira-Martins, J., S. Scarpetta, and D. Pilat. 1996. Mark-up pricing, market structure and the business cycle. *OECD Economic Studies* 27: 71–105.

Panagarya, A. 2005. Agricultural trade liberalization and the least developed countries: Six fallacies. *World Economy* 28: 1277–1299.

Piermartini, R., and R. Teh. 2005. Demystifying modeling methods for trade policy. Economic Research and Statistics Division, World Trade Organization, Geneva. Draft.

Polaski, S. 2006. *Winners and losers—Impact of the Doha Round on developing countries.* Washington, D.C.: Carnegie Endowment for International Peace.

Reimer, J. J. 2002. *Estimating the poverty impacts of trade liberalization.* GTAP Working Paper 20. West Lafayette, Ind., U.S.A.: Center for Global Trade Analysis, Purdue University.

Reitzes, J. D. 1991. The impact of quotas and tariffs on strategic R&D behaviour. *International Economic Review* 32 (4): 985–1007.

Sutton, J. 1991. *Sunk costs and market structure.* Cambridge, Mass., U.S.A.: MIT Press.

Takayama, T. 1967. International trade and mathematical programming. *Australian Journal of Agricultural Economics* 11: 36–48.

Takayama, T., and G. C. Judge. 1964. Equilibrium among spatially separated markets: A reformulation. *Econometrica* 32: 510–524.

Van der Mensbrugghe, D. 2005. Linkage technical reference document—Version 6.0. Development Prospects Group, World Bank, Washington, D.C. Mimeo.

Wainio, J., and J. Gibson. 2003. The significance of nonreciprocal trade preferences for developing countries. Paper presented at the International Conference on Agricultural Reform and the WTO: Where Are We Heading? Capri, June 23–26.

Wall, H. J. 1999. Using the gravity model to estimate the costs of protection. *Federal Reserve Bulletin, Federal Reserve Bank of St. Louis,* January–February: 33–40.

Winters, L. A. 2000. Trade policy as development policy. Presented at the UNCTAD X High-level Round Table on Trade and Development, Bangkok, February 12. Available at www.unctad.org.

Winters, L. A., N. McCulloch, and A. McKay. 2004. Trade liberalization and poverty: The evidence so far. *Journal of Economic Literature* 42: 72–115.

World Bank. 2002. *Global Economic Prospects: The developing countries: Making world trade for the world's poor.* Washington, D.C.

————. 2003. World development indicators. Available at http://publications .worldbank.org/WDI/.

————. 2004a. *Global Economic Prospects: Realizing the development promise of the Doha Agenda.* Washington, D.C.

————. 2004b. World development indicators. Available at http://publications .worldbank.org/WDI/.

About the Author

Antoine Bouët joined IFPRI in February 2005 as a senior research fellow in the Markets, Trade, and Institutions Division to conduct research on global trade modeling, trade policies, regional agreements, and multilateral trade negotiations. He is also professor of economics at the University of Pau, France.